BURNLEY
FOOTBALL CLUB:
The Complete A to Z

Dean Hayes

Published by Sigma Leisure – an imprint of
Sigma Press, 1 South Oak Lane, Wilmslow, Cheshire SK9 6AR, England.

British Library Cataloguing in Publication Data
A CIP record for this book is available from the British Library.

ISBN: 1-85058-680-2

Typesetting and Design by: Sigma Press, Wilmslow, Cheshire.

Cover Design: Sigma Press and MFP Design & Print

Cover photographs: top, from left – Wayne Biggins, Jimmy McIlroy, John Francis; bottom – John Angus, programme for 12 March 1960, Harry Potts.

Printed by: MFP Design & Print

Photographs: The photographs in this book have been supplied by the Lancashire Evening Post and from the author's personal collection.

Dedication

To Clarets fans everywhere!

Thanks to . . .

I should like to express my thanks to the following organisations for their help: Burnley FC; The Association of Football Statisticians; The Football League; The British Newspaper Library; The Harris Library Preston; and local libraries, Bolton, Burnley, Blackburn and Accrington. Thanks also to the following individuals Ben Hayes; Iain Price; Cyril Walker and Derek Lord.

Bibliography

Burnley FC – A Pictorial History of The Clarets by Tony Durkin, 1988

Burnley – A Complete Record 1882-1991 by Edward Lee and Ray Simpson

Up the Clarets - the Story of Burnley FC by David Wiseman, 1973

Let's talk about Burnley by Tom Morgan, 1946

Vintage Claret: A Pictorial History of Burnley FC by David Wiseman 1975

So you think you're a Claret – Official Burnley Quiz Book 1991

Football League Players' Records 1946-1992 by B.Hugman

ABANDONED MATCHES

During the 1908-09 season, Second Division Burnley beat Bristol Rovers (Away 4-2); Crystal Palace (Home 9-0 after a goalless draw) and Tottenham Hotspur (Home 3-1 after a goalless draw) to win a place in the fourth round of the FA Cup. The Clarets were drawn at home to reigning League Champions Manchester United. Heavy snow had fallen over Turf Moor and the chances of actually starting the game looked slim. However, the referee decided to get the contest underway and just before half time, Arthur Ogden gave Burnley the lead. In the second half, United laid siege to the Clarets' goal but a mixture of good luck and fine goalkeeping by Dawson kept their forwards at bay. Just when it seemed as if the Clarets were going to produce a major cup upset, the referee abandoned the game after 72 minutes with the snow making conditions underfoot almost unplayable.

In the replayed game two weeks later, Arthur Ogden scored twice but United ran out winners 3-2 and ended Burnley's cup run.

ADAMSON, JIMMY

Ashington-born Jimmy Adamson was snapped up by the excellent Burnley scouting system from East Chevington, turning professional on New Year's Day 1947. During his first few years at Turf Moor, Adamson was still playing as an inside-forward and it was only after he had been converted to wing-half that he began to realise his true potential.

He made his debut as a replacement for Reg Attwell in a 1-1 draw at Bolton Wanderers in February 1951 and, for the next 13 seasons, he was a virtual ever-present. Within three years he had won England 'B' honours when he played in the first-ever meeting with Scotland 'B' at Edinburgh. He also represented the Football League and although a full international cap eluded him, success at Turf Moor did not. He skippered the Clarets to the League Championship in 1959-60, being one of three ever-presents. Two years later he had his most memorable season, taking Burnley to the FA Cup Final where they lost to Spurs, being named Footballer of the Year and gaining inclusion in

Jimmy Adamson, who both played for and managed the Clarets

the World Cup squad for Chile, where he was assistant to England manager Walter Winterbottom. When Winterbottom resigned, Adamson was offered the England manager's job. He felt he couldn't accept the position because of his lack of managerial experience.

In February 1964, Jimmy Adamson played the last of his 486 games for Burnley in a 1-1 draw at Blackpool. Adamson became a coach at Turf Moor when he retired, being appointed manager six years later.

Though the club lost their First Division status in 1970-71, he led the Clarets to the Second Division Championship in 1972-73. They were unlucky not to win a place in Europe in 1973-74 after finishing sixth in Division One and reaching the semi-finals of the FA Cup. Adamson parted company with the club halfway through the 1975-76 relegation season and after a brief spell with Sparta Rotterdam, he became manager of Sunderland, replacing FA Cup hero Bob Stokoe. He was too late to prevent the Wearsiders sliding into Division Two and though they came close to returning to the top flight at the first attempt, they fell away. Adamson who had something of a love-hate relationship with Sunderland supporters, left the club in October 1978 to take over from Jock Stein as manager of Leeds United.

He took the Elland Road club into Europe and to a League Cup semi-final but after a poor start to the 1980-81 season he resigned and left the game for good.

AGGREGATE SCORE

Burnley's highest aggregate score in any competition came in the Texaco Cup first round match against East Fife in 1973-74 when they notched up 10 goals over the two legs. The Clarets won the first leg at Turf Moor 7-0 with Paul Fletcher netting a hat-trick and then won 3-2 at Bayview Park.

ANDERSON, JOE

Joe Anderson began his career in his native Scotland with Vale of Leven, later playing for Airdrieonians, Dumbarton and Clydebank. It was from the latter club that he joined Burnley in March 1920, making his debut in a 2-1 home win over Sunderland at the end of that month. He scored six goals in eight games as the Clarets finished runners-up to West Bromwich Albion in the First Division, including his first hat-trick for the club in a 5-0 home win over Everton.

When Burnley won the League Championship in 1920-21, Anderson was the club's top scorer with 25 goals in 41 games. Included in his total were five goals in a 7-1 defeat of Aston Villa and four in a 6-0 home win over Sheffield United. He also netted six goals in two FA Cup appearances, including four in a 7-3 win at Leicester City in the first round. His prolific partnership with Bob Kelly continued the following season when he again topped the club's scoring charts with 21 goals. After that both his and the club's performances were disappointing and in October 1923, after scoring 72 goals in 126 games, he rejoined Clydebank, later ending his career with Glasgow Pollock.

ANGLO-SCOTTISH CUP

The Anglo-Scottish Cup was inaugurated in 1975-76 following the withdrawal of Texaco from the competition of that name. Burnley didn't enter until 1976-77 but after the following results – Blackburn Rovers (Away 1-1) Blackpool (Away 1-2) and Bolton Wanderers (Home 1-0) failed to make the knockout stages. It was a similar story in 1977-78 for after beating Blackburn Rovers (Home 2-1) the Clarets lost 1-0 at Bolton Wanderers and 4-0 at home to Blackpool. It was a different story in 1978-79 as Burnley won the trophy. Unbeaten in their group games – Preston North End (Home 3-2) Blackpool (Home 3-1) and Blackburn Rovers (Away 1-1) – the Clarets met Celtic in the quarter-finals. A Steve Kindon goal gave Burnley a 1-0 victory in the home leg and the Clarets' winger along with Ian Brennan scored the goals in a 2-1 win at Parkhead. After the semi-final tie against Mansfield Town had ended all-square at 2-2 after the two matches, the Clarets won 8-7 on penalties. Burnley faced Oldham Athletic in the two-legged final and after winning 4-1 at Boundary Park were favourites to lift the trophy. Despite a 1-0 home defeat, Burnley won the cup 4-2 on aggregate.

In 1979-80, Burnley failed to win a group game – Blackburn Rovers (Away 2-2) Blackpool (Away 2-3) and Preston North End (Home 1-2) – and though their results were better the following season – Bury (Away 1-2) Oldham Athletic (Home 3-1) and Shrewsbury Town (Home 1-1), they still failed to qualify for the knockout stages.

ANGUS, JOHN

After playing his early football for Amble Boys' Club in the north-east of England, John Angus joined Burnley as an amateur in 1954 and signed professional forms on his 17th birthday in September 1955. Following injuries to a number of the club's key defenders, Angus made his Burnley debut in a 2-1 home win over Everton in September 1956 and went on to be the club's first-choice right-back for the next 15 seasons. During his time with Burnley, Angus won a League Championship medal in 1959-60 and an FA Cup runners-up medal in 1962. He was ever-present in 1962-63 when the club finished third in Division One.

Unfortunate to be around at the same time as Blackpool's Jimmy

Armfield, he won only one full cap for England when he played left-back against Austria in 1961, though he had won seven Under-23 caps and represented England Youth.

In a career that spanned three decades, Angus, who was one of the best right-backs in the top flight, represented the Football League and went on to appear in 521 League and Cup games for the Clarets, scoring four goals. Two of his strikes came in the same match in October 1964 as Burnley lost 3-2 to Arsenal.

When his playing days were over, he severed all connections with the game and went to live and work in Northumberland.

John Angus one of the best full-backs in the top flight.

APPEARANCES

Jerry Dawson holds the record for the greatest number of appearances in a Burnley side, with a total of 569 games to his credit between 1907 and 1928. In all, Dawson played in 522 league games and 46 FA Cup matches and one Charity Shield. The players with the highest number of appearances are:

	League	FA Cup	FLg Cup	Others	Total
Jerry Dawson	522	46	0	1	569
John Angus	438/1	45	25	12	520/1
Jimmy McIlroy	439	50	3	5	497
Martin Dobson	406/4	31	34	24	495/4
Jimmy Adamson	426	52	3	5	486
Tommy Cummings	434	38	6	1	479
Brian Miller	379	50	13	13	455
Fred Barron	400	23	0	0	423
Leighton James	331/5	17	22	27/1	397/6
George Waterfield	371	23	0	0	394

ASSOCIATE MEMBERS CUP

The early rounds of this competition announced by the Football League in December 1983 were run on knockout lines and played con a regional basis. One of the founder entrants, Burnley beat Bolton Wanderers 2-1 in the first round with goals from Donnachie and Biggins. The former Matlock Town forward was on target again in rounds two and three as Darlington (Home 2-1) and Doncaster Rovers (Away 3-1 after extra-time) were beaten. In the Northern Area semi-final, the Clarets travelled to Prenton Park to play Tranmere Rovers but lost 2-0 after extra-time.

ATTENDANCES – AVERAGE

The average home league attendances of Burnley over the last ten seasons have been as follows:

1988-89	7,062		1993-94	11,317
1989-90	6,222		1994-95	12,135
1990-91	7,882		1995-96	9,064
1991-92	10,521		1996-97	10,053
1992-93	10,537		1997-98	10,481

ATTENDANCE – HIGHEST

The record attendance at Turf Moor is 54,775 for the third round FA Cup game against Huddersfield Town on 23 February 1924. For the record, the Clarets won 1-0 with Walter Weaver scoring the all-important goal.

ATTENDANCE – LOWEST

The lowest attendance for a first-class match at Turf Moor is 1,138 for the Freight Rover Trophy preliminary round match against Darlington on 13 March 1986. For the record, Alan Taylor scored for the Clarets in a 1-1 draw.

ATTWELL, REG

The son of a professional footballer, Reg Attwell began his Football League career with West Ham United but during the Second World War 'guested' for Doncaster, Leeds and Burnley. He had impressed and when it was discovered that he was not a first team regular at Upton Park, Clarets' boss Cliff Britton had no hesitation in bringing him to Burnley.

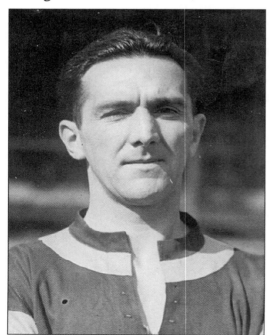

Reg Attwell

He made his debut in a 1-1 draw at home to Luton Town going on to appear in 22 games as the club won promotion to the First Division. He also played in that season's FA Cup Final when Burnley were beaten 1-0 by Charlton Athletic after extra-time. His consistency brought him international recognition in March 1949 as he played for the Football League against the Scottish League and he was most unfortunate not to have won full international honours for his country.

In December 1952, Attwell failed to turn up at Turf Moor for the match against Arsenal, having attended his father's funeral in Denaby. After that he shared the wing-half spot with Jimmy Adamson and it came as no surprise that after scoring 11 goals in 269 games he was transferred to Bradford City.

He spent just one season at Valley Parade before leaving to play in the Lancashire Combination for Darwen.

AUTOGLASS TROPHY

The Autoglass Trophy replaced the Leyland Daf Cup for the 1991-92 season. The Clarets won both of their group games, beating Blackpool 3-1 at Bloomfield Road and then defeating Doncaster Rovers 2-0 at Turf Moor. In the first round, Burnley entertained Scarborough but after a goalless ninety minutes, the referee abandoned the game due to frost, thus not allowing any extra-time. In the rearranged fixture, Burnley won 3-1 with goals from Conroy, Deary and Eli. In the Northern Area quarter-finals, the Clarets drew 1-1 at Rotherham United before winning 4-2 on penalties. A crowd of 10,775 saw Burnley beat Huddersfield Town 2-0 in the semi-finals and book a place in the Northern Area Final against Stockport County. The Clarets lost the first leg at Turf Moor 1-0 and though John Pender netted in the return at Edgeley Park, County won 3-1 on aggregate.

In 1993-94 Burnley went out of the competition in the first round, losing 2-1 at Preston North End.

AUTOWINDSCREEN SHIELD

Replacing the Autoglass Trophy for the 1994-95 season, the Clarets did not participate in the competition until the following season after their relegation from the First Division. The club drew both their group games against Rotherham United and Chester City 1-1, thus qualifying for the knockout stages where they met Crewe Alexandra. The only goal of the game was scored by Kurt Nogan in extra-time and took the Clarets through to the Northern Area quarter-final and a meeting with Carlisle United at Brunton Park. The Cumbrian side completely outplayed the Turf Moor club and won 5-0.

In 1996-97, Burnley won their first round match at Hartlepool United 2-0 but went out at the next hurdle, losing 1-0 at home to Stockport County.

In 1997-98, the Clarets got a bye into the second round where goals from Little and Cooke helped them beat Notts County 2-0. In the quarter-finals, Burnley defeated Carlisle United 4-1 to set up a semi-final meeting with Preston North End. The only goal of a hard fought game came in the 39th minute and was scored by Andy Payton. It was Payton who scored Burnley's goal in a 1-1 draw at Grimsby Town in the Northern Area Final first leg but the Burnley forwards seemed to have lost their shooting boots in the return leg, the Mariners winning 2-0 in front of a Turf Moor crowd of 10,257.

AWAY MATCHES

Burnley's best away wins have come in the FA Cup at Penrith on 17 November 1984 when the Clarets won 9-0 and against Keswick on 31 October 1903, though the match in which Burnley won 8-0, was switched to Turf Moor. The club's best win away from home in the League is 7-1 at Birmingham on 10 April 1926. The club have also scored seven goals on their travels at Leicester City (7-3 in 1920-21) and Newcastle United (7-2 in 1928-29).

The Clarets' worst away defeat came in the FA Cup competition of 1885-86 when they lost 11-0 at Darwen Old Wanderers. In the League Burnley have lost two games by a 10-0 scoreline, at Aston Villa on 29 August 1925 and Sheffield United on 19 January 1929.

AWAY SEASONS

The club's highest number of away wins came in seasons 1946-47, 1960-61, 1972-73 and 1991-92 when they won 11 of their 21 matches. With the exception of 1960-61 when the Clarets finished fourth in Division One, the club won promotion as champions or runners-up in each of the other three seasons.

In 1902-03, Burnley failed to win a single away game, drawing one and losing 16 of their matches!

B

BARRON, FRED

Fred Barron played his early football for his home-town club Stockton St Mary's before signing for Burnley in 1898. The tough-tackling right-half made his debut for the Clarets in a 1-1 draw at Sheffield United on 1 October 1898, after which he missed very few games over the next 12 seasons, being ever-present in 1900-01, 1902-03, 1903-04 and 1906-07.

At the beginning of the 1902-03 season, Barron was appointed club captain but his first season ended with the club bottom of the Second Division and having to apply for re-election. During his time at Turf Moor, the Clarets were in the main, a mid-table club and never challenged for honours until after Barron had left. Following the signing of Jack Cretney from Newcastle United in 1905, Barron moved to right-back, continuing to give dependable performances for the Turf Moor club.

He lost his place in the Burnley side during the 1910-11 season to the former Cowdenbeath defender Bob Reid and after scoring 14 goals in 423 League and Cup games decided to retire.

BEEL, GEORGE

The greatest goalscorer in the club's history, George Beel had an unsuccessful trial with Manchester United before signing for Lincoln City. After spells with Merthyr Town and Chesterfield, Beel left the Spireites to join Burnley in April 1923. His first game for the club came in the final match of the 1922-23 season when the Clarets lost 2-0 at home to Birmingham. The following season Beel established himself in the Burnley first team alongside Kelly and Cross and was the club's top scorer with 21 goals including his first hat-trick for the club in a 5-1 home win over West Ham United. He continued to find the net on a regular basis over the next three seasons but in 1926-27 when the club finished fifth in Division One, Beel netted three hat-tricks against Newcastle United (Away 5-1) Bolton Wanderers (Home 4-3) and Tottenham Hotspur (Home 5-0) in his total of 27 goals. The following season despite Burnley's poor showing in the League, Beel established a new club seasonal total of 35 goals, hitting hat-tricks in the wins over Derby County (Home 4-2) and Sheffield United (Home 5-3). He had another successful season in 1928-29, netting four hat-tricks in his total of 32 goals in victories over Newcastle United (Away 7-2) Birmingham (Away 6-3) Portsmouth (Home 4-1) and Leeds United (Home 5-0). The last of his 11 hat-tricks for the club came in February 1931 as the Turf Moor club beat Wolves 4-2. Beel, who was the club's top scorer in six of his nine seasons at Turf Moor, scored 187 goals in 337 games, 178 of them in the Football League.

He was allowed to leave Turf Moor in February 1932 and returned to play for Lincoln City before moving to Rochdale seven months later where he ended his league career. In the summer of 1933 he moved into non-league football as the player-manager of Tunbridge Wells Rangers.

BELLAMY, ARTHUR

After impressing in the club's Central League Championship successes of 1961-62 and 1962-63, Arthur Bellamy was given his first team debut in March 1963 when he scored one of the goals in Burnley's 5-2 win over Manchester City at Maine Road. In his first appearance for the Clarets in 1963-64, Bellamy scored a marvellous hat-trick in a 4-3 win at Everton. Though he was never an automatic choice in his ten seasons with the club, Bellamy gave the Clarets great service, going on to play in 250 League and Cup games. Not a prolific scorer, his 29 goals included another hat-trick in a 6-1 home win over Orient in September 1971.

He left Turf Moor in the summer of 1972 to play for Chesterfield. In three seasons with the Saltergate club he scored 12 goals in 133 league games before rejoining Burnley. He had spells as the youth and reserve team coach and as the club's assistant-manager before becoming head groundsman.

BENSON, JOHN

John Benson joined Manchester City as an amateur in 1958 before turning professional three years later. After making 44 appearances he moved to Torquay United and later Bournemouth where he was made captain by John Bond. In fact, he seemed to spend most of his career following Bond about. He played alongside him at Torquay, played under him at Bournemouth and Norwich City and coached under him at Manchester City and Burnley.

In February 1983, Benson took over from Bond at Maine Road, something he could never have thought possible when City let him go in the summer of 1964. He did not survive long at Maine Road for after Luton won three on the last day of the season to send City into the Second Division, he was sacked.

He teamed up with Bond at Turf Moor and when the Burnley manager departed, he took over the reins. The Clarets finished 21st in the Third Division, beating Rotherham United 7-0 and Penrith 9-0 in the FA Cup but with Fourth Division football beckoning, he resigned. He later worked as chief scout for Barnsley but his now back in management with Wigan Athletic.

BERESFORD, MARLON

Goalkeeper Marlon Beresford was on Sheffield Wednesday's books when he was loaned out to Bury where he made his Football League debut. Further loan spells with Ipswich Town, Northampton Town and Crewe Alexandra followed before Burnley paid £95,000 to bring the talented 'keeper to Turf Moor.

Throughout the 1992-93 season, Beresford was in outstanding form, saving four of seven penalties awarded against the club and beings elected for the PFA divisional team as the best 'keeper in the Second Division. When the club won promotion to the First Division via the play-offs in 1993-94, Beresford played in every match and again won a PFA award as the division's top goalkeeper. He continued to give outstanding displays week in, week out for the Clarets and so it came as no surprise when a number of Premiership clubs showed an interest in him. It was around this time that he began to suffer from a series of injuries, notably a hernia operation and a bad back. Once fully recovered, he was ever-present in the Burnley side in the 1997-98 season until his transfer to Middlesborough for £500,000. Beresford, who could have left for nothing at the end of the season had played in 294 games for the Clarets.

BEST START

Burnley were unbeaten for the first 16 games of the 1972-73 season when they won the Second Division Championship. They won seven and drew nine of those matches before losing 2-1 at home to Orient on 11 November 1972.

BIGGINS, WAYNE

After scoring on his league debut for Lincoln City in March 1981, he was rather surprisingly released and moved into non-league football, first with King's Lynn and then Matlock. Burnley signed him in February 1984 and he made his debut in a 2-2 home draw against Brentford. In only his fourth appearance for the club, he netted a hat-trick in a 4-0 home win over Lincoln City, the club that had let him go. The following season, despite the club being relegated to the Fourth Division, Biggins top scored with 18 goals. He was still finding the net in the league's basement when Norwich City paid £40,000 for his services in October 1985.

Biggins, who had scored 43 goals in 101 games, helped the Canaries win the Second Division Championship in his first season at Carrow Road but then found goals hard to get in the top flight and in July 1988, he joined Manchester City. He helped the Maine Road club win promotion to the First Division before leaving to sign for Stoke City.

He was the Potters' top scorer for three consecutive seasons with his 22 goals in 1991-92 the best of his career. He then moved to Barnsley where he again top-scored and after a brief spell with Celtic, he rejoined Stoke City. After a loan spell with Luton Town he moved to Oxford before joining Wigan Athletic in January 1996 and helped the Latics win the Third Division Championship.

BLACKLAW, ADAM

Aberdeen-born goalkeeper Adam Blacklaw joined Burnley in 1954 and made his debut for the Clarets in a 6-2 home win over Cardiff City on 22 December 1956 following an injury to Colin McDonald. He played in 11 games over the next two seasons but then made the position his own following the injury McDonald sustained whilst playing for the Football League, an injury that ended his career. When Burnley won the League Championship in 1959-60, Blacklaw played in all but one game, his performances leading to him winning international recognition, making two appearances for the Scotland Under-23 side. After missing just one game again in 1960-61, Blacklaw was ever-present in seasons 1961-62, 1962-63 and 1963-64, appearing in 172 consecutive league games. He won three full caps for his country, the first against Norway in 1963.

Blacklaw, whose first team place came under threat from Harry Thomson, appeared in 383 League and Cup games for Burnley before leaving to join Blackburn Rovers in July 1967. He spent three seasons at Ewood Park, appearing in 96 league games before moving to end his first-class career with Blackpool. However, he only played in one league game for the Bloomfield Road club – as a replacement for Harry Thomson!

He then played non-league football for Great Harwood Town before managing Clitheroe.

BOLAND, ALF

Alf Boland was the youngest secretary in the Football League when he was chosen by Burnley to replace the departed Albert Pickles in November 1932. Boland, who had played for the club's junior sides whilst working in the office of a textile mill in the town, was appointed secretary-manager in 1935.

He shared team responsibilities with the board and was never in sole charge at Turf Moor. Boland was in fact, more of an administrator than an out-and-out football man and was also a regular contributor to the club's programme. He left the club just after the Football League closed down at the start of the Second World War.

BOND, JOHN

John Bond made his name as an outspoken manager after a career as a full-back for West Ham United and Torquay United. A dead-ball expert, especially from the penalty-spot, he scored eight goals in the Hammers' Second Division Championship winning season of 1958-59 and played in the club's 1964 FA Cup Final victory over Preston. At Torquay he helped them to promotion to Division Three before his retirement in 1969. He went into management first with Bournemouth, then Norwich City, winning success for both clubs.

In October 1980 he joined Manchester City and in his first season at Maine Road he led them to the League Cup semi-finals and the FA

Cup Final where they lost to Spurs in a replay. At the start of the 1982-83 season, Bond and his assistant Benson refused offers to work for Benfica but after a good start, City faltered and in February 1983, Bond resigned.

In June 1983, he was appointed manager of Burnley when many Clarets' fans expected Frank Casper to gave been given the job on a permanent basis. Bond brought in players he'd had under him at previous clubs and though the season started well for him, it fell away following the injury to Kevin Reeves at the turn of the year and the Clarets had to settle for 12th place. Bond departed in the close season, later managing Swansea, Birmingham and Shrewsbury Town.

Always attracting the attention of the media, he was fined by the FA in 1987 for allegedly bringing the game into disrepute following some unflattering remarks about the England coaching scene.

Bond was so unpopular with the Turf Moor faithful that in December 1992 he heeded police advice to stay away from Shrewsbury's game there!

BOWES, BILLY

Inside-forward Billy Bowes joined Burnley from Scottish junior club Broxburn in February 1891 and made his league debut the following month in a 6-2 home win over Preston North End. Over the next ten seasons, Bowes missed very few games and was ever-present in 1894-95. When the club finished bottom of the First Division in 1896-97, Bowes was the top-scorer with 11 goals and netted the opening goal in the club's only success in that seasons Test Matches. Their failure to win more than one game meant that the Clarets would be playing Second Division football for the first time in their history in 1897-98. Forming a good understanding with Walter Place junior, he helped provide a number of chances for Ross and Toman as the Clarets won the Championship and gained promotion via the Test Matches.

Bowes went on to score 84 goals in 295 games before leaving Turf Moor to work at the Bank Hall pit, whom he helped win the Burnley Hospital Cup in 1904.

BOYLE, TOMMY

Tommy Boyle is the only Burnley captain to lift the FA Cup, when it was presented to him by King George V following the Clarets 1-0 victory over Liverpool at the Crystal Palace in 1914.

One of the most powerful headers of a ball, Tommy Boyle began his league career with his local club Barnsley and after establishing himself in the Oakwell club's side, was made captain. He led the Yorkshire club to the 1910 FA Cup Final where they lost to Newcastle United in a hard fought match.

In September 1911, Burnley splashed out a club record fee of £1,150 to bring Boyle to Turf Moor and he made his debut for the Clarets on the last day of the month in a 1-1 draw at Barnsley!

Within a matter of weeks, Boyle had been appointed the Clarets' captain and in his first season with the club led them to third place in Division Two. In 1912-13 he captained the club to promotion to the First Division and to the semi-final of the FA Cup, where despite him scoring his fourth goal of the competition, the Clarets lost 3-2 to Sunderland in a replay. His performances led to him winning international recognition when he played for England against Ireland in Belfast. The following season he was part of the famous half-back line of Halley, Boyle and Watson that not only helped the club consolidate their position in the top flight but also win the FA Cup.

Despite suffering serious injuries whilst fighting in France during the First World War, Boyle lined up in the Burnley side for the first match of the 1919-20 campaign before scoring the club's first goal that season in a 1-1 draw at Bolton in the following match. In 1920-21, Boyle captained the Clarets to the League Championship as they went a record 30 games without defeat.

He went on to score 43 goals in 236 League and Cup games before leaving to become player-coach at Wrexham. He later coached in Germany before returning to live in Blackpool where sadly his health deteriorated and following a nervous breakdown, he was under medical treatment for the rest of his life.

BRADSHAW, HARRY

Harry Bradshaw was appointed as Burnley's secretary in 1891 before becoming chairman two years later after Arthur Sutcliffe had succeeded him as secretary.

In 1896 he replaced Sutcliffe as the club's team manager but in his first season in charge, the Turf Moor club finished bottom of Division One and after playing in the Test Matches were relegated for the first time in their history. After persuading Jimmy Ross to leave Liverpool, he and Wilf Toman scored the goals that helped the club win the Second Division Championship and promotion after the Test Matches. In 1898-99 after bringing goalkeeper Jack Hillman back to Turf Moor, the club finished third in the top flight but after losing the services of Ross and Toman, he too left Burnley to become manager of Woolwich Arsenal.

When he arrived at Highbury, the club was on the verge of bankruptcy, but he quickly transformed it to win promotion back to Division One. He left the Gunners in 1904 to become Fulham's first full-time manager. He took the Craven Cottage club to two Southern League titles and eventually into the Football League. In 1907-08 the Cottagers reached the FA Cup semi-finals and narrowly missed promotion to the First Division. In 1909 he became the secretary of the Southern League, a position he held until his death in 1921.

BRAY, GEORGE

Wing-half George Bray played his early football with Great Harwood Town before joining Burnley in October 1937. After some impressive performances in the club's Central League side, he made his first team debut in a 3-2 home win over Luton Town in October 1938. He played in the remaining 34 games that season and then appeared in 59 wartime games for the club before resuming his league career with the Clarets in 1946-47. Also during the hostilities he 'guested' for Glentoran and appeared for them in the Irish Cup Final of 1942.

When Burnley won promotion to the First Division in 1946-47, Bray missed just one game – a 1-0 defeat at Nottingham Forest – one of only six defeats that season. He also helped the Clarets reach that season's FA Cup Final where they lost 1-0 to Charlton Athletic. An ever-present in seasons 1947-48 and 1950-51, Bray played in 259 League and Cup games scoring nine goals before spending a season in the club's Central League side. He then joined the club's coaching staff and after spells as the 'A' team and reserve team trainer, stepped up to train the first team. He later worked as the Clarets' kit man before retiring in 1992.

BRENNAN, IAN

Ian Brennan signed professional forms for the Clarets in 1970 and, though he impressed in the club's Central League side whilst playing as a forward, he made his league debut at left-back as Burnley lost 4-0 at Stoke City. The following season of 1974-75 saw Brennan win a regular place in the Burnley side and on 24 September 1974 he scored his first goal for the club in a 1-0 win at Liverpool. His strike from fully 30 yards beat England 'keeper Ray Clemence all ends up to give the Clarets the points and prevent the Anfield club from returning to the top of the table. Despite a series of solid performances, Brennan faced stiff competition from Keith Newton in 1975-76 and only played in two matches. The following season Newton moved to right-back and Brennan re-established himself in the Clarets' side.

He missed very few games over the next four seasons but in December 1980 after scoring 14 goals in 211 games, he left Turf Moor to join Bolton Wanderers.

Sadly, the Easington-born defender was plagued by injuries during his time at Burnden Park and made only 17 appearances in his two years with the club. He later played for both Burnley Belvedere and Colne Dynamoes before hanging up his boots.

BRITTON, CLIFF

Cliff Britton was a footballing genius who was later to turn his talents to management. He arrived at Everton in 1930 after beginning his career with Bristol Rovers. A cultured wing-half whose passing ability was second to none, he played in the Everton side that beat Manchester City in the 1933 FA Cup Final and won the first of nine England caps against Wales in 1934. He went on to play in 240 League and Cup games for the Blues but when the club won the League Championship in 1938-39, he played in only one game, being an adviser to the reserve team.

During the Second World War, his career enjoyed something of a revival as he won 12 wartime caps, forming a fine England half-back line with Cullis and Mercer.

After the war had ended, he took charge of Burnley and in February 1946 at the club's annual general meeting, announced that he had developed a promotion programme that would see the Clarets back in the top flight within three years. He achieved this in his first season with the club and took them to the FA Cup Final where they lost 1-0 to Charlton Athletic. After guiding the Clarets to third place in Division One, he returned to Everton as manager. In 1953-54 he took the Goodison club back to the top flight following their relegation in 1950-51 but in 1956 a dispute arose over the club wanting to appoint an acting manager while Britton was abroad with the team, so he parted company with them.

BROMILOW, TOM

Liverpool-born Tom Bromwilow was invalided out of the army during the First World War, went to Anfield and asked for a trial. Within two years he was playing for England. He made his league debut in October 1919 and went on playing until 1930, making 374 appearances and winning two League Championship medals in 1922 and 1923. Bromilow was a fine left-half who won the first of his five England caps in 1921 in a goalless draw against Wales, having earlier played for the North team that beat an England XI 6-1.

When he retired he took up a coaching position in Amsterdam but returned a year later to embark on a highly successful managerial career.

When he took over as manager of Burnley, the Clarets just missed out on relegation to the Third Division in 1933. After that they were a mid-table side but did reach the semi-finals of the FA Cup in 1935 when they lost 3-0 to Sheffield Wednesday at Villa Park. He left Turf Moor at the end of that season to take charge at Crystal Palace but resigned in June 1936 after a row with the directors. He was reappointed six months later, Palace finishing as runners-up in the Third Division (South) in 1938-39.

He left Selhurst Park to manage Leicester City, where his sides won the Midland Cup in 1941 and the War League South in 1942. In 1948 he managed Newport County but he left the club two years later with them heading for re-election.

BROTHERS

David Walders joined Burnley from Barrow in the summer of 1903 and made his debut in the heart of the Clarets' defence in a goalless draw at Chesterfield on the opening day of the 1903-04 season. The following campaign, his brother Jack followed him from Holker Street and when the two of them played against West Bromwich Albion (Home 1-4) at the start of the 1904-05 season, it was the first time that two brothers had played in the same Burnley side.

Whilst there have been other brothers who have played for the Clarets, the only pair that have appeared in the same Burnley side other than the Walders are Vince and Richard Overson. Vince Overson helped Burnley to win the Third Division Championship in 1982 and appeared in 261 games for the club. The two brothers lined up together for the first time on 3 November 1979 when the Clarets lost 2-1 at home to Orient. In fact, they appeared in the same Burnley team on five occasions in that relegation season and were never on the winning side!

BROWN, ALAN

Alan Brown began his playing career with Huddersfield Town before 'guesting' for Liverpool, Manchester United and Notts County during the Second World War. In 1945 he was selected as reserve for the England team to play Scotland at Villa Park.

In February 1946 he joined Burnley and was immediately appointed captain. After making his debut in a 1-1 home draw against Coventry City he went on to be ever-present as the club won promotion to the First Division. He also captained the club in the FA Cup Final at Wembley where they lost 1-0 to Charlton Athletic. He won his only representative honour whilst with the Clarets when he captained the Football League to a 4-3 win over the Irish League in Belfast in 1948. He had made 98 appearances for Burnley before leaving to play for Notts County. He joined Sheffield Wednesday as coach in 1951 before returning to Burnley as manager in 1954. After finishing in mid-table in his first season, the club finished seventh in both 1955-56 and 1956-57 but at the end of the latter campaign, he left to join Sunderland.

He led the Wearsiders back to the top flight in 1963-64 but rather than enjoy his new success, he moved to Sheffield Wednesday as manager. He took the Owls to the FA Cup Final of 1966 but two years later was back at Roker Park. Sunderland were relegated in 1969-70 but despite them challenging for promotion, Brown lost his job and after coaching in Norway, assisted Plymouth Argyle before retiring.

BROWN, JIM

A Scottish Schoolboy international, he played part-time football for a number of junior clubs before joining East Fife. In 1927 he helped the Bayview Park club reach the Scottish Cup Final where they were beaten by Celtic. He left the Scottish League club at the end of that season to join Burnley, making his debut in a 2-0 defeat at West Ham United in October 1927. In his first season with the Turf Moor club, he made a number of appearances at centre-half before settling into the side at right-half.

Brown was a first team regular for eight seasons, scoring five goals in 241 League and Cup games. He left Turf Moor in the summer of 1935 to join Manchester United, helping the Old Trafford club win promotion to the First Division at the end of his first season. He appeared in 110 first team games for the Reds before leaving to end his League career with Bradford Park Avenue.

BROWN, JOE

Joe Brown began his Football League career with Middlesborough before arriving at Turf Moor in the summer of 1952. He made his debut for the Clarets in a 1-1 home draw against Chelsea but after just six league appearances, a slipped disc put him in hospital for a lengthy time. After making a comeback in the reserves, he joined Bournemouth and in six years at Dean Court, he appeared in 215 League games for the Cherries.

Whilst on the south coast, he had qualified as an FA coach and after a short spell with Aldershot, he retired from playing to take up a position as Burnley's third team coach. In 1968 he was instrumental in the club's youngsters winning the FA Youth Cup and the following year was appointed chief coach. In January 1976 after three years as Jimmy Adamson's assistant, he replaced him when Adamson resigned in 1976. The 1975-76 season ended with relegation to Division Two and he was unable to stop the slide the following season, losing his job in February 1977.

Within six months he was back in the game as Youth Development Officer with Manchester United, later Youth Administrator.

BRUTON, JACK

A former pit lad, Jack Bruton began his playing career with Horwich RMI and then had trials with Bolton Wanderers. However, it was at Turf Moor that he established himself as one of the best wingers in the country – it was reported that he came up from the pit and signed professional forms on an overturned tub at the pit head.

He scored on his league debut, though the Clarets lost 3-1 at home to Newcastle United. A maker of goals as well as a scorer, Bruton proved to be remarkably consistent during his playing career with the Clarets. In 1927-28 his accurate crosses provided George Beel with a number of goalscoring opportunities during his record breaking season. Bruton, who had already represented the Football League, won the first of three full international caps for England when he played against France in 1928. He had scored 44 goals in 176 games for the Clarets when he was allowed to leave Turf Moor in December 1929 and join Blackburn Rovers who paid a club record fee of £6,500 for his services.

He spent ten seasons as a player at Ewood Park, appearing in over 300 games. On retirement, he remained with Rovers as assistant-trainer and secretary. When Will Scott was dismissed as manager, Bruton took over the reins. However, he couldn't prevent the club being relegated and he took steps in an attempt to bounce straight back by signing Dennis Westcott, a proven goalscorer for Wolves. Rovers finished in mid-table and Bruton was sacked. He later managed Bournemouth but after six seasons at Dean Court, he severed all connections with the game.

BUCHAN, MARTIN

By the time Martin Buchan arrived at Old Trafford from Aberdeen for a fee of £125,000 in March 1972, he was already a Scottish Footballer of the Year, a Scottish Cup winner and an international. He had won his first cap in 1972 against Portugal and went on to win 34 caps over the next seven years.

Buchan was an outstanding defender and leader. He had been captain of Aberdeen by the age of 20 and it was not long before he was carrying out a similar task at Old Trafford. He went on to give 12 seasons loyal service, making 455 appearances. He was captain of the United side that lifted the FA Cup in 1977, making him the first player since the war to captain a Scottish and English Cup-winning side. On top of his Cup winners' medals, he also picked up two losers' medals and a Second Division Championship medal. He left Old Trafford in 1983 to join Oldham Athletic but retired after just one season.

In June 1985 he was appointed manager of Burnley but after only four months in charge, he left Turf Moor, unable to make the transition from player to manager.

CAPACITY

The total capacity of Turf Moor in 1998-99 was 22,546.

CAPS

The most capped player in the club's history is Jimmy McIlroy who won 51 caps for Northern Ireland.

CAPS (ENGLAND)

The first Burnley player to be capped by England was James Crabtree when he played against Ireland in 1894. The most capped player is Bob Kelly with 11 caps.

CAPS (NORTHERN IRELAND)

The first Burnley player to be capped by Northern Ireland was Tom Morrison who played against Wales in 1899. The most capped player is Jimmy McIlroy with 51 caps.

CAPS (SCOTLAND)

The first Burnley player to be capped by Scotland was Jock Aird when he played against Norway in 1954. The Glencraig-born full-back is also the most capped player with four caps.

CAPS (WALES)

The first Burnley player to be capped by Wales was Stan Bowsher when he played against Northern Ireland in 1929. The most capped player is Brian Flynn with 33 caps.

CAPTAINS

Among the many players who have captained the Clarets is Tom Boyle, the only Burnley skipper to have lifted the FA Cup. Having been signed from his home-town team of Barnsley for £1,150, he led Burnley to promotion from the Second Division in 1912-13 and the following season, captained the club as they beat Liverpool 1-0 in the FA Cup Final. After the hostilities he was still the Clarets' skipper and in 1920-21 he led the club to the First Division Championship, creating a record that still stands today of 30 games without defeat.

Alan Brown joined Burnley from Huddersfield Town in 1946 and in his first season with the club led them to promotion to the First Division and to a place in that season's FA Cup Final where sadly they lost 1-0 to Charlton Athletic.

Jimmy Adamson was captain of the Burnley side when they won the League Championship for a second time in 1959-60. In 1962 he was voted Footballer of the Year and led the Clarets out at Wembley where they went down 3-1 to Spurs in that seasons FA Cup Final.

Martin Dobson captained Burnley's Second Division Championship-winning team of 1972-73 and in 1981-82 during a second spell with the club, skippered the side to the Third Division Championship.

Other notable captains have included Mick Docherty who captained the Clarets to FA Youth Cup success in 1968; Peter Noble who led the club to victory in the Anglo-Scottish Cup of 1978 and Ray Deakin who led the Clarets out at Wembley in the Sherpa Van Trophy Final of 1988. The club's last successful captain was John Pender who took the Clarets to the Fourth Division Championship in 1991-92.

CASPER, FRANK

Frank Casper began his Football League career with Rotherham United and had scored 26 goals in 102 league games for the Millers when he was sold to Burnley for £30,000 in the summer of 1967.

Frank Casper – another Claret who played for and managed the Turf Moor club

He scored on his debut as the Clarets beat Coventry City 2-1 at home on the opening day of the 1967-68 season and ended the campaign as the club's top scorer with 14 goals. He led the way again in 1968-69 and scored six goals in the club's run to the League Cup semi-finals. He continued to score goals throughout his Turf Moor career with a best of 18 in 1971-72. When Burnley won the Second Division Championship in 1972-73, Frank Casper was ever-present, contributing 12 goals to the club's success.

His performances led to him representing the Football League but sadly his career was brought to a premature end when following an injury sustained at Leeds United in March 1974, he was forced to miss the entire 1974-75 campaign. He tried a comeback but after scoring 89 goals in 275 games he had to retire.

He then became Burnley youth team coach, later holding that position with the reserves and first team. In January 1983 he became caretaker manager but left six months later to become assistant-manager to Martin Dobson at Bury. He returned to Turf Moor in January 1989 and managed the club until September 1991, when he resigned following unrest amongst the supporters.

CAVANAGH, TOMMY

One of the game's more colourful characters, Tommy Cavanagh appeared for six League clubs in a 12-year playing career. He 'guested' for Preston North End during the Second World War, signing professional forms for the Deepdale club in 1949. He did not make a league appearance for the Lilywhites and left to play for Stockport County. His next port of call was Huddersfield Town whom he helped win promotion to the First Division in 1952-53. He later played for Doncaster Rovers, Bristol City and Carlisle United before a short spell as player-manager of Cheltenham Town. He was trainer, then manager of Brentford and coach at Nottingham Forest before joining Tommy Docherty at Hull City.

When Docherty became manager of Manchester United, he took Cavanagh with him. He was assistant-manager to Dave Sexton at Old Trafford, a position he later held at Newcastle before joining the coaching staff of Wigan Athletic. In 1985 he was appointed as Burnley's trainer by Martin Buchan but when the Scottish international resigned just three months into the season, Cavanagh took over. The club ended the campaign in 14th place but in June 1986 he resigned due to ill-health.

CENTRAL LEAGUE

The Central League was formed in 1911 by the Northern and Midland giants of the Football League as a reserve team league. The first-ever winners were not, however giants, but Lincoln City – who won it with 48 points out of a possible 64 before immediately withdrawing from the League.

Up until 1981-82, there was just one League and Burnley secured the Championship on three occasions – 1948-49; 1961-62 and 1962-63. From 1982-83 there were two divisions but in 1986 after two finishes in next to the bottom of the League, the club decided not to seek re-election. After the three seasons, the club had a change of heart and decided to apply for re-election to the Central League and were successful. Following the decision to restructure the Pontins League into four divisions, Burnley found themselves in Division Two and in 1997-98 won the Championship.

CENTURIES

Six players have scored 100 or more league goals for the Clarets. George Beel is the greatest goalscorer with 178 strikes in his Burnley career (1923-1932). Other centurions are Ray Pointer(118); Jimmy

McIlroy (116); Louis Page (111); Bert Freeman (103); and Andy Lochhead (101).

Only two players have made over 100 consecutive league appearances for the club immediately following their debuts – Jimmy Strong 203 and Ray Deakin 102. Three other players have made over 100 consecutive league appearances during their careers. They are Adam Blacklaw (172) Tommy Cummings (127) and Alan Stevenson (127).

CHAMPIONSHIPS

Burnley have won a divisional championship on six occasions. The first time was in 1897-98 when the club were unbeaten at home and in fact, only lost two of their 30 matches to win the Second Division title. Promotion was not automatic and Burnley had to play in the Test Matches before taking their place in the top flight. After finishing runners-up in the First Division in the first season following the First World War, the Clarets won the League Championship in 1920-21. After losing their opening three games, Burnley embarked on a 30-match unbeaten run which remains a record for the top flight to this day.

The club won the League Championship again in 1959-60. On 2 May Burnley defeated Manchester City 2-1 at Maine Road to go to the top of the First Division for the first time in the season and became champions by a point from Wolverhampton Wanderers. They had lost 6-1 to Wolves on 30 March 1960. To achieve the title, Burnley had to take five points from their last three games and the final one was played when the other contenders had completed their programme.

In 1972-73 the Clarets were unbeaten in their opening 16 matches and after losing just four throughout the campaign, won the Second Division Championship, one point ahead of runners-up Queen's Park Rangers.

Burnley's fifth divisional Championship success came in 1981-82. The Clarets lost six of their opening eight fixtures before losing just two of their next 38 games and taking the title on goal difference from Carlisle United.

The club's last Championship success was in 1991-92 when they won the Fourth Division title, finishing six points ahead of Rotherham United.

The 1959-60 League Championship winning side.
Back: Cummings, Miller, Elder, Blacklaw, Seith, Angus.
Front: Connelly, McIlroy, Adamson, Pointer, Robson and Pilkington

CHARITY SHIELD

Burnley have appeared in the FA Charity Shield on three occasions:

1921	v Tottenham Hotspur at White Hart Lane	0-2
1960	v Wolverhampton Wanderers at Turf Moor	2-2*
1973	v Manchester City at Maine Road	1-0

* Trophy shared, each club retaining it for six months.

CHEESEBROUGH, ALBERT

Though Albert Cheesebrough made his Burnley debut in April 1952 as a 17-year-old as the Clarets drew 1-1 with Manchester United, he only appeared in 13 league games over the next four seasons. It was 1955-56 before he became a first team regular, his performances earning him selection for the England Under-23 side against France. He formed a fine left-wing partnership with Brian Pilkington but when Jimmy Robson appeared on the scene in 1958-59 Cheesebrough lost his place. His total of 40 goals in 158 games included a hat-trick in a 7-3 home win over Leicester City, the club that paid £20,000 for his services in the summer of 1959.

During the Filbert Street club's run to the FA Cup Final in 1961, Cheesebrough was the Foxes' leading scorer but by the time they appeared in the final again in 1963, Cheesebrough was not in the side. He joined Port Vale for a then club record fee of £15,000 before later ending his league career with Mansfield Town, managed by Tommy Cummings.

CHEW, JACKIE

Jackie Chew was an amateur with his home-town team Blackburn Rovers in 1939 but during the war he 'guested' for Leeds United, Burnley and Luton Town. When the hostilities were over, he signed for Burnley and made his league debut in the 1-1 draw against Coventry City on the opening day of the 1946-47 season. He soon developed a fine understanding with inside-right Billy Morris and the two of them helped the club win promotion to the First Division and appear in that season's FA Cup Final. In 1948-49, Chew was the club's leading scorer with 11 goals and went on to score 41 in 248 games before being transferred to Bradford City in the summer of 1954.

After just one season at Valley Parade, he returned to Lancashire to team up with former team-mate Reg Attwell at Darwen.

CLEAN SHEETS

This is the colloquial expression used to describe a goalkeeper's performance when he does not concede a goal. Alan Stevenson in 1980-81 kept 20 clean sheets from 44 League appearances, helping the Clarets to finish eighth in Division Three.

COATES, RALPH

Ignored by the professional clubs, Ralph Coates took a job at Eppleton Colliery and it was whilst playing for the Colliery's Welfare side that he was noticed by Burnley. He made his league debut in a 3-1 home win over Sheffield United in December 1964. A tireless, bustling worker who could be back defending one minute and looking to score the next, Coates quickly established a reputation as a more than promising winger/wide midfield player. His performances soon earned him international recognition and in his time at Turf Moor he won eight England Under-23 caps, played four

Ralph Coates, mid-field player who won England international honours whilst with the Turf Moor club.

times for the Football League and won two England caps. The first of these came against Northern Ireland in April 1970. Sadly, like many of his talented team-mates, Coates who had scored 32 goals in 261 games, was allowed to leave the Clarets for economic reasons.

He joined Tottenham Hotspur for £190,000 and his first appearances as a Spurs player were his third and fourth caps for England against Malta and Wales at Wembley in May 1971.

At White Hart Lane, Coates never truly completed the spectacular development that earned him star billing at Turf Moor. A member of the Spurs team that won the UEFA Cup in 1972, his crowning moment came in the 1973 League Cup Final against Norwich City when as a substitute he thumped home the winning goal. He left Spurs in 1978 to play for the old St George's club of Sydney but later returned to play for Orient.

He played non-League football for Hertford Heath, Ware and Nazeing before becoming the manager of a Hertfordshire leisure complex.

COLLINS, DOUG

Though he joined Rotherham United as an apprentice, Doug Collins began his Football League career with Grimsby Town and had scored 11 goals in 100 games by the time of his £30,000 move to Burnley in September 1968. Collins had impressed the Burnley officials during that season's second round of the League Cup when the two sides drew 1-1 at Blundell Park before the Clarets won 6-0 in the replay.

Collins made his Burnley debut wearing the Number 2 shirt in a 2-1 home win over Chelsea, though over the season he wore five different numbered shirts before becoming the club's first-choice inside-left. In that 1968-69 season, Collins was very impressive but then fell away for three seasons before re-establishing himself in the side in 1972-73 as the club won the Second Division Championship.

After two more seasons with the Clarets in the top flight, Doug Collins, who had scored 19 goals in 217 games, left Turf Moor to join Plymouth Argyle. After later playing for Sunderland and coaching Derby, he became player-manager of Rochdale. He later emigrated to Australia where he combined coaching with a number of business interests.

COLOURS

In their early days, Burnley were known as 'The Hornets' because they played in amber and black shirts. However, they soon changed to blue and white stripes before in the early 1900s, switching to green shirts. At the start of the 1910-11 season, the club decided to adopt the colours of a successful top flight club and chose the claret and blue of Aston Villa. Though there have been occasions when Burnley have worn white or blue for home games, the club's colours are still claret and blue.

CONNELLY, JOHN

John Connelly joined the Clarets from his home-town team, St Helens Town in 1956 but remained an amateur until he had completed his apprenticeship as a joiner at the age of 21. He made his first team debut in a 1-1 draw at Leeds United in March 1957. It was immaterial as to which flank the notably two-footed Connelly occupied. He was direct and always seeking to have a shot on goal and was one of the top-scoring wingmen in the game throughout the late fifties and early sixties.

He was a member of the Turf Moor club's Championship-winning side of 1959-60, scoring 20 goals in 34 games. His form that season led to him winning the first of 20 full caps for England when he played in a 1-1 draw against Wales at Ninian Park.

One of his best goals for the club came in the following season's European Cup competition against Rheims in France. Carrying the ball from inside his own half, he evaded one or two desperate lunges before unleashing a powerful shot from fully 25 yards. Connelly also netted two hat-tricks for the Clarets against Fulham (Away 5-3) in 1961-62 and Manchester United (Away 5-2) in 1962-63. He went on to score 105 goals in 265 games before joining Manchester United for £60,000 in April 1964.

In his first campaign at Old Trafford he scored 15 goals, helping United to win the Championship and thus collect his second Championship medal. He hammered in one of the goals in March 1966 as the much-vaunted 'Eagles of Lisbon' had been completely outplayed and beaten 5-1 by United.

He last appeared for England in the opening match of the 1966 World Cup Finals in a goalless draw against Uruguay. After two years at Old Trafford, in which he scored 35 goals in 113 games, he left to join Blackburn Rovers for a fee of £40,000.

He continued to find the net, scoring 36 goals in 149 league games for Blackburn before ending his Football League career with Bury and retiring to take over a fish and chip shop.

CONROY, MIKE

Glasgow-born forward Mike Conroy began his career as an apprentice with Coventry City but having failed to make the grade, returned to Scotland to play for Clydebank. After a short spell with St Mirren, he signed for Reading for £40,000. He spent three seasons at Elm Park playing in both midfield and defence before joining the Clarets in the summer of 1991. He scored on his league debut on the opening day of the season as Burnley lost 2-1 at Rotherham United. He continued to find the net throughout the season as the Clarets won the Fourth Division Championship. His total of 24 goals in 38 games included a hat-trick in a 4-1 home win over Gillingham. Unfortunately he was unable to recapture his prolific scoring powers of the previous season in 1992-93 and after being unable to agree terms early the following season, signed for Preston North End after scoring 39 goals in 99 games for the Clarets.

In two seasons at Deepdale, Conroy scored 24 goals in 72 games before joining Fulham in the summer of 1995. He was the Cottagers' leading scorer in 1995-96 and in 1996-97 became the first Fulham player to hit 20 goals in a season since Gordon Davies. His contribution to the club's promotion won him a place in the PFA divisional team. Surprisingly he was sold to Blackpool for a fee of £50,000 in March 1998.

CONSECUTIVE HOME GAMES

Burnley played a sequence of six home League and Cup games in succession between 29 January 1898 and 12 March 1898. The Clarets were undefeated with the following results:

Date	Opponents	Competition	Score
29.01.1898	Woolwich Arsenal	FA Cup Round 1	3-1
05.02.1898	Small Heath	Division 2	4-1
12.02.1898	Burslem Port Vale	FA Cup Round 2	3-0
05.03.1898	Burton Swifts	Division 2	2-0
07.03.1898	Newton Heath	Division 2	6-3
12.03.1898	Gainsborough Trinity	Division 2	1-1

CONSECUTIVE SCORING – LONGEST SEQUENCE

Ray Pointer and Willie Irvine hold the club record for consecutive scoring in the Football League, being on target in seven consecutive league games. Their records are:

Ray Pointer 1958-59		Willie Irvine 1965-66	
Aston Villa(Home 3-1)	1 goal	Leeds United(Away 1-1)	1 goal
Newcastle.U(Away 2-5)	2 goals	West Ham Utd(Home 3-1)	2 goals
Spurs(Home 3-1)	1 goal	Sunderland(Away 4-0)	1 goal
Man City(Away 4-1)	2 goals	Aston Villa(Home 3-1)	1 goal
Leicester.C(Away 1-1)	1 goal	Liverpool(Away 1-2)	1 goal
Leicester.C(Home 3-3)	2 goals	Spurs(Home 1-1)	1 goal
Leeds Utd(Home 3-1)	1 goal	Fulham(Away 5-2)	3 goals

CROSS, BENNY

An England Schoolboy international, Benny Cross joined Runcorn following an FA tour of Canada immediately after the First World War. His outstanding performances helped Runcorn to win the Cheshire County League Championship in 1919-20, his only season with the club. He joined Burnley in April 1920 but had to wait until the fourth match of the following season before making his debut in a 3-0 home win over Huddersfield Town. He missed just two more games that season as the Clarets, following his debut, embarked on a 30-match unbeaten run that helped them win the League Championship.

Though not a prolific scorer, that 1920-21 season was Cross' best in terms of goals scored, the Birkenhaed inside-forward finding the net 14 times in 37 games. He missed very few matches over the next six seasons and was ever-present in 1922-23 when he netted his only hat-trick for the club in an 8-2 home win over Nottingham Forest. His form in this, one of the club's most successful periods, led to him making an appearance for the Football League against the Scottish League at Filbert Street, but injury curtailed his career and at the end of the 1927-28 season, after which he had scored 61 goals in 255 games, he was forced to retire.

CUMMINGS, TOMMY

Tommy Cummings, who was one of the fastest defenders in the game, made his Football League debut for the Clarets in a 2-2 draw at Manchester City in December 1948. With the exception of a two-year spell when the popular defender suffered from a series of injuries, Cummings was a virtual ever-present in the Burnley side for 11 seasons.

He represented the Football League in 1951 and won three England 'B' caps in 1953 and 1956. Though full international honours eluded him, he came very close in 1950 when he was selected as reserve for the game against Ireland in Belfast.

Though he faced stiff competition from Brian Miller during the club's 1959-60 League Championship-winning season, Cummings played in the last eight games of the campaign alongside Miller, with Bobby Seith the man to miss out. He was in the Burnley side that lost to Spurs in the 1962 FA Cup Final. Cummings went on to play in 479 games and though he only scored three goals, one of them was amongst the best goals ever scored at Turf Moor. Burnley's opponents were Newcastle United in a match that stood at 1-1 with just six minutes remaining. Cummings dispossessed the Magpies' England international centre-forward Jackie Milburn on the edge of the Burnley penalty area and moved forwards, evading a number of tackles until he entered the Newcastle half. With no-one in support, he kept going forward until beating Newcastle captain Joe Harvey just outside the Magpies' penalty area and unleashing an unstoppable left-foot drive into the roof of the net for the winning goal.

Cummings was chairman of the PFA for two years before he took over as player-manager of Mansfield Town. He almost led the Stags to promotion in his first season but in the summer of 1967 he was appointed manager of Aston Villa. He spent 16 largely undistinguished months at Villa Park and in November 1968 with the club languishing at the bottom of the Second Division, he was sacked.

DAVIS, STEVE

Steve Davis joined the Clarets on loan from Southampton in November 1989, not having appeared in the Saints' league side. He made his debut for Burnley as a substitute for Paul Atkinson in a 1-0 defeat at Lincoln City but after nine outings he returned to The Dell where he eventually appeared in the top flight for Southampton.

In August 1991, Burnley manager Frank Casper paid £60,000 to bring David to Turf Moor on a permanent basis and in his first season with the club, his partnership with John Pender at the heart of the Burnley defence was instrumental in the Clarets winning the Fourth Division Championship. Not surprisingly his performances earned him a place in the PFA's Fourth Diviison 'Team of the Season'. A virtual ever-present, Davis helped the Clarets win promotion for a second time in three years when they beat Stockport County in the play-off final at Wembley. He took over the club captaincy, but when the Clarets were relegated after just one season in the First Division,

Davis, who had scored 25 goals in 221 games, joined Luton Town for a club record incoming fee of £750,000.

Davis was appointed the Hatters' captain and in his second season with the club was elected to the PFA Second Division XI by his fellow professionals. In his third season at Kenilworth Road, he won the Players' Player of the Year award and took his total of goals to 17 in 143 games before returning to Turf Moor for a second spell.

DAWSON, JERRY

The holder of the club record for the greatest number of appearances, goalkeeper Jerry Dawson played his early football for Portsmouth Rovers whilst serving an apprenticeship to the Cliviger blacksmith. He joined Burnley in 1907 and made his debut in a 3-0 win over Stockport County in April 1907. It was his only appearance that season but from 1907-08, Dawson became the club's first-choice 'keeper for the next 15 seasons either side of the First World War.

In 1910, he represented the Football League against the Scottish League at Ewood Park and again the following year in the return match at Ibrox Park. In 1912-13 he helped the club win promotion to the First Division and reach the FA Cup semi-finals. The following season the club reached the FA Cup Final but unfortunately Dawson twisted a thigh muscle in a goalless draw against Sheffield United in the semi-final at old Trafford. The Clarets won the replay 1-0 and though Dawson reappeared in the side for a league game against Manchester City which Burnley lost 4-1, he bruised his ribs and decided he wasn't sure of lasting out the 90 minutes in the final.

When league football resumed in 1919-20, Dawson was still in goal for the Clarets as they finished the season as runners-up in the First Division. The following season despite being injured in the 4-1 defeat at home to Bradford City, he recovered to play in 39 games as the club won the League Championship for the first time in their history.

Dawson's form in that Championship-winning season led to the Burnley 'keeper winning the first of two full caps for his country in a 1-1 draw against Ireland in Belfast the following October.

Jerry Dawson went on to play in 569 League and Cup games for the club, making his last appearance at the age of 40 years 282 days on Christmas Day 1928 as the Clarets beat Liverpool 3-2.

DEAKIN, RAY

Ray Deakin began his career with Everton and was ever-present in their Central League side, although he failed to appear for the first team. In the summer of 1981 he joined Port Vale but he was often played out of his familiar left-back position. After one season at Vale Park he joined Bolton Wanderers on a free transfer. He became a regular in the Bolton side and despite the Trotters' relegation to the Third Division, he kept his place, being made captain for a spell. Following the emergence of Jimmy Phillips, he moved into the centre of defence and took his total of appearances to 121 before joining Burnley in May 1985.

Following his debut for the Clarets in a 3-2 home win over Northampton Town on the opening day of the 1985-86 season, Deakin was the club's only ever-present. He was ever-present again the following season, captaining the side in the game against Orient that was vital for the club's survival and made 102 consecutive league appearances from his debut.

In 1988, Deakin became the first Burnley captain since Jimmy Adamson in 1962 to lead the side out at Wembley as the Clarets played Wolves in the Sherpa Van Trophy Final. The following season he suffered a series of injuries and missed much of the campaign. He returned to full fitness and was a member of the Clarets' first team for the next two seasons, taking his total of appearances to 271 before being released.

DEARY, JOHN

John Deary began his Football League career with Blackpool, making his debut in a 2-1 win at Fulham in September 1980 and played in 10 games as the Seasiders were relegated to the Fourth Division at the end of that campaign. The Blackpool management seemed uncertain whether to play him in midfield or in the heart of defence. Eventually the Ormskirk-born player settled into midfield and in 1984-85 when the Bloomfield Road club won promotion, he top-scored with 13 goals in 31 games. Deary spent ten years with the Seasiders, scoring 53 goals in 341 games before joining Burnley for £30,000 in the summer of 1989.

He made his debut as a substitute at Rochdale on the opening day of the 1989-90 season before winning a regular place in the club's midfield. In 1990-91, he helped the Clarets to the Fourth Division play-offs and then the following season was one of the most influential members of Burnley's Fourth Division Championship winning side. During his five seasons at Turf Moor he was a virtual ever-present and in 1993-94, his last full season with the club, he helped the Clarets reach the First Division via the play-offs. He had scored 30 goals in 291 League and Cup games when he was transferred to Rochdale for £25,000 in January 1995.

He played in 106 games for the Spotland club before being released in the summer of 1997.

DEBUTS

Ian Lawson scored four goals for Burnley on his debut on 5 January 1957 as the Clarets beat Chesterfield 7-0 in an FA Cup third round tie at Turf Moor. Tom Nicol scored a hat-trick on his debut against Preston North End in March 1891. Goalkeeper Billy O'Rourke's debut at Queen's Park Rangers on 27 October 1979 wasn't quite as happy. The giant 'keeper conceded seven goals in a match that featured on 'Match of the Day'! Leigh Palin only appeared in one game for the Clarets, a 1-0 defeat at Bradford City on 11 October 1992, thus becoming the first player in the club's history to make his League debut on a Sunday. In comparison to Billy O'Rourke's televised debut, full-back Wayne Dowell made his debut in a live televised game against Sheffield United on 20 November 1994, a game in which the Clarets won 4-2.

DEFEATS – FEWEST

During the 1972-73 season, the Clarets went through a 42-match programme and suffered only four defeats in winning the Second Division Championship.

DEFEATS – MOST

Burnley's total of 23 defeats during the 1975-76 season is the worst in the club's history. Not surprisingly they finished 21st in the First Division and were relegated.

DEFEATS – WORST

Burnley's record defeats was in the club's pre-League days when they lost 11-0 to Darwen Old Wanderers in an FA Cup first round match on 17 October 1885. In the Football League, the Clarets have twice suffered 10-0 defeats at Aston Villa on 29 August 1925 and at Sheffield United on 19 January 1929.

DEFENSIVE RECORDS

Burnley's best defensive record was established in 1897-98 and helped the club win the Second Division Championship. They conceded just 24 goals in that campaign and were beaten in just two matches. The Clarets' worst defensive record was in 1925-26 when they let in 108 goals in finishing 20th in the First Division.

DERBIES

Burnley and Blackburn Rovers were among the original 12 members of the Football League, but the two clubs had first met at Turf Moor on 27 September 1884 in front of a 5,000 crowd. Unfortunately for the Clarets, Rovers ran out winners 4-2. Burnley were not long in gaining revenge, for in March 1885 they won 5-1 on the same ground. The first meeting in Blackburn took place at Leamington Road and ended all-square at 2-2.

The first league match between the clubs was at Turf Moor on 3 November 1888, the game producing a 7-1 win for Blackburn. The following season, Rovers won their home fixture by the same margin and in 1890-91 beat Burnley quite handsomely. Things certainly couldn't get much worse for the Clarets and after a 3-3 draw at Ewood Park, they finally recorded their first league success on 12 December 1891, beating Blackburn 3-0 at Turf Moor. However, the game was not without controversy. In driving snow and with a strong wind behind them, Burnley raced into a 3-0 lead at the interval. Early in the second-half, Burnley's Stewart and Blackburn's Lofthouse were sent-off after a brief altercation to be followed by all the outfield players of the Blackburn team! This left the ten men of Burnley against the Rovers' 'keeper Herbie Arthur who immediately appealed for offside as they bore down on his goal! Wisely, the referee abandoned the game and the points were awarded to Burnley.

The following season saw the beginning of the old First Division and the club's first meeting in it was goalless, though over the next few seasons, it was Rovers who had the upper hand, winning five consecutive matches at Ewood Park from 1892-93. However, in the final game of the 1895-96 season, Burnley beat Blackburn 6-0 at Turf Moor with Tom Nicol grabbing a hat-trick for the Clarets.

The clubs next met in the Test Match series at the end of the 1897-98 season as Rovers had finished next to the bottom of the First Division and Burnley had won the Second Division Championship following their relegation the previous season. Burnley won both matches with Wilf Toman scoring a hat-trick in the first.

It was after the First World War when the derby matches really came into their own. In 1920-21 Burnley won the League Championship and did the 'double' over Rovers, winning 4-1 at Turf Moor and 3-1 at Ewood Park. During the 1920s, three Blackburn players, McIntyre, Rigby and Harper all netted hat-tricks in this fixture. After the Clarets were relegated in 1929-30 it was another six years before the two clubs met again and followed Rovers' relegation to the Second Division. The club's first meeting in the Second Division was goalless but Rovers won the return 3-1 with Jack Bruton scoring for the Ewood Park club. Bruton, who scored for Burnley against Rovers in the 1920s, is the only player to have scored for both clubs against the other.

Rovers won the Second Division Championship in 1928-39 and after Burnley won promotion in 1946-47, the clubs resumed their meetings in the top flight. But as the Clarets took three points from their meetings, Rovers were relegated and it was to be 1958-59 before the sides met again. Burnley had the better of things over the coming seasons and won four games in succession at Ewood Park, culminating in Rovers being relegated in 1965-66.

The two clubs didn't meet again until 1976-77 when Burnley won four of the six games over the next three seasons with Peter Noble netting in four of them. Despite both clubs entering the Third Division during this time, they managed to avoid playing each other in that section and met in the League for the last time in 1982-83. Sadly, Rovers did the double over the Clarets who were relegated.

Though the clubs have never met in the League Cup, they have played each other on five occasions in the FA Cup. The honours are even with each side winning twice and one encounter, which was probably the most exciting game between the clubs, ending as a draw. The first FA Cup meeting saw Burnley, who were then a Second Division club beat Rovers from the First Division at EwoodPark on 8 March 1913, 1-0 with Tommy Boyle scoring the all-important goal. The second meeting in 1952 produced a 3-1 win for Blackburn with the Ewood Park club then the Second Diviison 'underdogs'. Burnley won the third meeting 2-1 before the clubs met for the fourth time in the FA Cup at Turf Moor on 12 March 1960.

After a goalless first-half, Burnley hit three goals in quick succession through Pilkington, Pointer and Connelly and appeared to be coasting to victory when the referee awarded a penalty to Rovers as the ball appeared to strike Elder's hand as it flew up from his boot. Douglas converted the spot-kick and then three minutes later, Peter Dobing unleased a powerful 20-yard shot past the unsighted Blacklaw in the Burnley goal, There were just four minutes left when Mick McGrath's half-hit shot found its way into the Burnley net for the equaliser. The replay at Ewood Park was a bad-tempered affair and though John Connelly was thwarted in the dying seconds by a fine Harry Leyland save, the game went into extra time where goals from Dobing and McLeod gave Rovers victory.

Burnley's record against Blackburn Rovers is as follows:

	P.	W.	D.	L.	F.	A.
Football League	80	33	13	34	141	149
FA Cup	5	2	1	2	7	9
Total	85	35	14	36	148	159

DISMISSALS

Whilst a number of Burnley players have received their marching orders over the years, perhaps the most famous of all is the dismissal of Billy Elliott in the match against Manchester City at Maine Road on 12 March 1952. The England international was sent-off after the infamous 'look of intent' incident in a game the Clarets won 1-0 courtesy of a Les Shannon goal.

In terms of the opposition players being dismissed, the match against Cambridge United on 24 November 1979 should perhaps take centre stage. After beating Blackburn Rovers 2-1 away on 14 April 1979, Burnley had a run of 24 league games without a win. They ended the sequence in the match against Cambridge, winning 5-3 but only after their opponents had two players sent-off just before the interval and five booked by the referee. The half-time score was 2-2 but the Clarets went ahead after the break with an own goal. Cambridge drew level again but Burnley scored twice in the last four minutes!

DRAWS

The Clarets played their greatest number of drawn league matches in a single season in 1981-82 when 17 of their matches ended all-square and their fewest in seasons 1891-92, 1892-93, 1893-94, 1894-95, 1900-01 and 1953-54 when only four of their matches were drawn.

The club's highest scoring draw is 4-4, a scoreline in nine games – Aston Villa (Away 1890-91); Burslem Port Vale (Away 1906-07); West Ham United (Away 1932-33); Sunderland (Away 1955-56); Tottenham Hotspur (Away 1960-61); Chelsea (Home 1960-61); Stoke City (Away 1963-64); Norwich City (Home 1975-76); and Charlton Athletic (Home 1976-77).

DOBSON, MARTIN

Martin Dobson started his career as a centre-forward with Bolton Wanderers but in 1967 they gave him a free transfer. He considered giving up the game but his father persuaded Burnley manager Harry Potts to give him a trial at Turf Moor. Dobson joined the Clarets as a front runner, making his debut in a 3-2 defeat at Wolves in September 1967. Eventually he was switched to midfield where he won international recognition, being called up for England Under-23s against Bulgaria at Plymouth. In 1972-73 he captained Burnley to the Second Division Championship and the following season led them to sixth place in Division One and to the semi-finals of the FA Cup. Four days after the semi-final, he won the first of five full international caps in a goalless draw against Portugal. In August 1974, Dobson moved to Goodison Park for £300,000, a new British transfer record.

He made his debut for the Blues in a 2-1 home win over Arsenal and in five years on Merseyside he was always a first team regular. He played in two UEF Cup campaigns, the 1977 FA Cup semi-final defeat by Liverpool and the League Cup Final against Aston Villa which the Midlands' side won after three matches. The 1978-79 League Cup campaign, he scored a hat-trick when Everton achieved their best scoreline, 8-0 against Wimbledon. It was something of a surprise when Dobson returned to Turf Moor in the summer of 1979 for £100,000 after scoring 40 goals in 230 League and Cup games for the Blues.

After failing to halt the Clarets' slide to the Third Division, he once again captained the club and in 1981-82 led them to the Third Division Championship. After scoring 76 goals in 499 games, he moved to Bury in 1984, later becoming player-manager and then manager of Bristol Rovers. He is now Youth Development Officer for his first club, Bolton Wanderers.

DOUGALL, BILLY

Billy Dougall joined Burnley from Falkirk in February 1926 for a fee of £3,000 and made his debut in a 1-1 draw at Everton. Over the next three seasons he played in 63 games for the club, his only goal coming in the 2-1 win over Cardiff City on Christmas Eve 1927.

In 1929 he joined Burnley's training staff after being forced to give up the game through injury. He started the youth development scheme at Turf Moor in the 1930s when the Clarets were one of the first clubs to set up such an organisation. He became the club's manager in the summer of 1957 following the departure of Alan Brown but was in the post for less than a year, relinquishing the position due to ill-health.

E

ELDER, ALEX

Signed from Irish League club Glentoran, left-back Alex Elder made his Burnley debut in a 1-0 defeat at Preston North End in September 1959 when he marked Tom Finney out of the game. He kept his place for the rest of the season, helping the Clarets win the League Championship. His consistency in the Burnley defence was rewarded when he won the first of 40 caps for Northern Ireland, playing against Wales in April 1960.

Over the next seven seasons, Elder, who formed a formidable full-back partnership with John Angus, was a virtual ever-present, though a broken ankle in pre-season training kept him out of the side for the first half of the 1963-64 season.

He was later appointed club captain, going on to score 17 goals in 330 games before becoming unsettled and asking for a transfer. In August 1967 he joined Stoke City for £50,000 and over five seasons at the Victoria Ground, appeared in 83 League games. His career with the Potters was marred by a series of injuries, though when he left the club in 1973, he continued to play, turning out for non-League Leek Town.

EUROPEAN CUP

After receiving a bye in the first round, Burnley's second round opponents in the 1960-61 European Cup competition were Stade De Reims who were considered one of the top clubs in Europe. The Clarets entry into European football could hardly have been more dramatic as Jimmy Robson scored after just 45 seconds. Burnley through Jimmy McIlroy added a second goal just minutes from time to give them a 2-0 lead to take to France. There is little doubt that the key to victory had come in the fact that Reims' star player Kopa, had been brilliantly man-marked by Walter Joyce. In the second leg, Kopa didn't play, the reason given being injury, but there were those who thought his absence was because he knew he couldn't beat the Burnley defence. Robson extended Burnley's lead before Reims scored two quick goals early in the second-half. John Connelly levelled the scores on the night but with 10 minutes to go, Reims again took the lead. After that Burnley somehow held on to record a famous 4-3 aggregate win.

In the quarter-final, Hamburg SV visited Turf Moor, bringing with them an unbeaten league record of having won 16 and drawn one of their 17 matches played. However, they were no match for the Clarets that night as two goals from Pilkington and another from Robson gave Burnley a 3-0 lead before Hamburg scored what was thought to be a consolation goal in the 75th minute. In the second leg in Germany, Hamburg ran out winners 4-1 against a depleted Burnley side to win the tie 5-4 on aggregate.

EVER-PRESENTS

There have been 75 Burnley players who have been ever-presents throughout a Football League season. The greatest number of ever-present seasons by a Burnley player is four with Tom McLintock, Joe Taylor, Fred Barron, Jimmy Strong and Alan Stevenson all achieving the feat.

EYRES, DAVID

Winger David Eyres was playing Northern Premier League football for Rhyl when Blackpool manager Jimmy Mullen paid £10,000 for his

services in the summer of 1989. His first season in league football ended in disappointment as the Seasiders were relegated to the Fourth Division. The club reached the play-off finals in both 1991 and 1992, winning promotion after beating Scunthorpe United in a penalty shoot-out in this latter season. In the 'new' Second Division, Eyres was the club's leading scorer with 16 goals. This led Eyres' former manager Jimmy Mullen to pay £90,000 to bring him to Turf Moor in July 1993.

The Clarets won promotion via the play-offs in 1993-94 and Eyres was the club's top scorer with 19 goals. He also scored seven goals in cup matches including a hat-trick in a 4-1 FA Cup win over Rochdale. In what was a prolific goalscoring campaign for the Liverpool-born player, he also netted the Clarets' opener in the 2-1 play-off final win

David Eyres, versatile Claret who was the club's top scorer in the promotion-winning season of 1993-94.

over Stockport County. Over the next few seasons he showed his versatility by playing at left-back, wing-back or central striker as well as his normal left-wing role and in 1996-97 he was selected in the PFA Second Division side for the season. He went on to score 55 goals in 215 games for the Clarets before leaving to join Preston North End for £80,000 in October 1997.

F

FA CUP

Burnley first competed in the FA Cup in the 1885-86 season but were barred from playing any of their large number of Scottish stars for the tie against Darwen Old Wanderers. Fielding their entire reserve team, they lost their first ever FA Cup tie 11-0.

It was 1908-09 before the club embarked on an FA Cup run of note, beating Bristol Rovers, Crystal Palace and Tottenham Hotspur before losing 3-2 to Manchester United after the original tie had been abandoned with Burnley leading 1-0. During the club's promotion-winning season of 1912-13, Burnley reached the FA Cup semi-finals for the first time in their history. After beating Leeds City (Away 3-2) Gainsborough Trinity (Home 4-1) Middlesborough (Home 3-1) and Blackburn Rovers (Away 1-0), the Clarets met Sunderland at Bramall Lane. In a closely fought semi-final replayed neither side could find the net and the game had to be replayed at St Andrew's four days later. This time the Wearsiders proved too strong, beating Burnley 3-2.

The following season the club went one better and reached their first FA Cup Final. Victories over South Shields (Home 3-1) Derby County (Home 3-2) Bolton Wanderers (Home 3-0) Sunderland (Home 2-1 after a goalless draw) paired the Clarets with Sheffield United in the semi-final. After a goalless draw at Old Trafford, a Tommy Boyle goal in the replay at Goodison Park took Burnley to the Crystal Palace for the final against Liverpool. Although the match was not an entertaining one, it was certainly historic, for among the 72,778 spectators was the reigning monarch King George V. It was the first time the sovereign had attended the Cup Final. The first-half belonged to Liverpool but Nicol the Reds' centre-forward missed two great chances. The only goal of the game came in the 58th minute when Burnley's Bert Freeman from a throw-in near the corner flag, volleyed the ball into the Liverpool goal with tremendous power.

The Clarets reached the semi-final stage again in 1923-24 and 1934-35 before losing 3-0 respectively to Aston Villa (at Bramall Lane) and Sheffield Wednesday (at Villa Park).

The club reached their first Wembley final in their Second Division promotion-winning season of 1946-47. After beating First Division high flyers Aston Villa 5-1, the Clarets reached their sixth semi-final with victories over Coventry City (Home 2-0) Luton Town (Home 3-0 after a goalless draw) and Middlesborough (Home 1-0 after a 1-1 draw). The semi-final against Liverpool also went to two matches before Ray Harrison scored the only goal of the game to take Burnley into the final against Charlton Athletic. It was the first FA Cup Final to be televised 'live' and though Charlton won the game 1-0 after extra-time, the Clarets missed a good number of opportunities in front of goal. Future manager Harry Potts crashed a shot against the crossbar but unfortunately the ball bounced to safety.

During the 1955-56 competition, Burnley were involved in four matches against Chelsea before the Stamford Bridge club progressed to the fifth round. The following season, Ian Lawson scored four goals on his debut as Chesterfield were beaten 7-0 and then Lawson and Jimmy McIlroy netted hat-tricks in a 9-0 win over New Brighton, Burnley eventually going out of the competition in the sixth round to Aston Villa after a replay.

In 1960-61, the Clarets again reached the semi-final stage only to be beaten 3-0 by Tottenham Hotspur at Villa Park as the White Hart Lane club went on to complete the 'double'. The following season, Burnley reached their second Wembley final, beating Queen's Park Rangers (Home 6-1) Leyton Orient (Away 1-0 after a 1-1 draw) Everton (Home 3-1) Sheffield United (Away 1-0) and Fulham 2-1 in the semi-final at Filbert Street after the original tie at Villa Park had ended all-square at 1-1. In the final, Burnley met Spurs and got off to a dreadful start when Jimmy Greaves put the London club ahead after three minutes. The Clarets equalised in the 49th minute through Jimmy Robson but within a minute Bobby Smith had restored Spurs' lead. Spurs added a third eight minutes from time when Danny Blanchflower scored from the penalty spot following Tommy Cummings' handball.

During the 1965-66 competition, Andy Lochhead established a new club record when he scored five goals in Burnley's 7-0 win over Bournemouth.

Burnley last reached the semi-final stage in 1973-74 when they lost 2-0 to Newcastle United at Hillsborough. In 1984-85, the Clarets equalled their best FA Cup score when they beat Penrith 9-0 with both Kevin Hird and Alan Taylor scoring hat-tricks.

FA CUP FINALS

The Clarets have appeared in three FA Cup Finals, winning the trophy on just one occasion.

1914	v Liverpool at Crystal Palace	1-0
1947	v Charlton Athletic at Wembley	0-1*
1962	v Tottenham Hotspur at Wembley	1-3

*After extra-time.

FARRELL, ANDY

Andy Farrell joined Burnley from his home-town club Colchester United after playing in 105 league games for the Layer Road club. He made his Burnley debut against his former club at Turf Moor on the opening day of the 1987-88 season, a game the Clarets lost

3-0. Farrell missed just one game during his first season with the club as they ended the season in 10th place in the Fourth Division. He was a member of the Burnley side that lost to Wolverhampton Wanderers in that season's Sherpa Van Trophy Final. In his first two seasons, Farrell played in midfield but following injuries to Gardner and Monington he moved into the centre of defence alongside Steve Davis. When John Pender arrived from Bristol City, Farrell was switched to sweeper, occasionally reverting to his former midfield role.

He was an important member of Burnley's Fourth Division Championship-winning side of 1991-92 and went on to score 25 goals in 349 League and Cup games before being allowed to join Wigan Athletic in September 1994. He played in 53 league games for the Latics before being released at the end of the 1995-96 season when he joined Rochdale.

FATHER AND SON

Brian Miller has given the club great service as a player, coach, manager and chief scout. The Burnley-born wing-half made his debut during the club's FA Cup marathon tie against Chelsea in 1956 and went on to help the Clarets win the League Championship in 1959-60. His form led to him being capped by England at full international level against Austria in Vienna in May 1961. He appeared in 455 games for the Clarets, later having two spells as the club's manager.

His on David played his first game for the club against Sheffield Wednesday on New Year's Day 1983 when his father who was manager at the time, sent him on to replace Derek Scott. Unable to win a permanent place in the Clarets' side, he had a loan spell at Crewe before later playing for Tranmere Rovers and Preston North End. In February 1989 he returned to Turf Moor for a brief loan spell before joining Carlisle United.

Walter Joyce joined Burnley straight from school, making his first team debut at Manchester City in August 1960. Over the next four seasons, he was an important member of the squad, though never a regular. He captained the club's Central League side to successive Championships in 1961-62 and 1962-63 but left Turf Moor in February 1964 to play for Blackburn Rovers. He later played for Oldham Athletic before becoming manager of Rochdale, after which he coached at a number of north-west clubs. His son Warren Joyce began his league career with Bolton Wanderers before joining Preston North End. After topping the Deepdale club's scoring charts in 1989-90, he signed for Plymouth Argyle but after just one season at Home Park he returned to the north-west to play for Burnley. Joyce, who cost £150,000, scored twice on his debut in a 2-1 win over Port Vale. He went on to appear in 90 games for the Clarets before leaving to play for Hull City where he is now the Yorkshire club's player-manager.

FINES

During the 1960-61 season, Burnley were fined £1,000 for fielding ten reserves in a First Division game against Chelsea. Four days after the encounter with the Stamford Bridge club, the Clarets were due to travel to play SV Hamburg in the third round of the European Cup and so wanted to rest the majority of their first team players. For the record, Burnley's 'reserves' drew 4-4 at home to Chelsea with Lochhead and Harris scoring two goals apiece whilst the club's interest in the European Cup ended with a 4-1 defeat in Germany after they had won the first leg 3-1.

FIRST DIVISION

Burnley have had six spells in the First Division. Founder members in 1888-89, the club spent nine seasons in the top flight before relegation in 1896-97 via the Test Matches. After winning promotion, again via the Test Matches at the first attempt, Burnley began their second spell in the First Division in 1898-99. After just two seasons the club were relegated again and did not return to top flight action until 1913-14. In 1919-20 the club finished the season as runners-up to West Bromwich Albion but the following season won the League Championship for the first time in their history. The club lost just one home game 4-1 to Bradford City on the opening day of the season and put together a 30-match unbeaten run which remains a top flight record. The Clarets were relegated at the end of the 1929-30 season and had to wait until 1947-48 before regaining their place in the First Division. This was the club's longest spell in the top flight, the 24 seasons bringing another League Championship success in 1959-60. After relegation in 1970-71 when the club only won seven of their games, the Clarets had another two years to wait before winning back their place in the top flight. But in 1975-76 after three seasons of First Division football, the club finished 21st and were relegated.

Following reorganisation in 1992-93, the club found themselves playing in the 'new' First Division in 1994-95 but at the end of the season, they were relegated.

FIRST LEAGUE MATCH

Burnley's first Football League game was played at Deepdale on 8 September 1888 against their Lancashire rivals, Preston North End. The home side raced into an early two-goal lead with Fred Dewhurst scoring the first after just two minutes. Many sources claim this to be the League's first goal but as the game only kicked off at 3.50.pm due to Burnley's late arrival, this is not so. Within a minute of that goal, Jack Gordon finished off a flowing movement to put North End 2-0 up. Burnley battled on and reduced the arrears before the interval when Pat Gallocher scored a fine opportunist's goal. Early in the second-half, Jimmy Ross, who was later to play for the Clarets, scored two goals in quick succession. Burnley to their credit never gave up the fight and Fred Poland scored a second goal for them. Dewhurst added a fifth for Preston who ran out winners 5-2 in an entertaining game played in brilliant sunshine.

The Burnley team was: W.Smith; A.Lang; W.Bury; J.Abrams; D.Friel; J.Keenan; A.Brady; W.Tait; F.Poland; P.Gallocher; and J.Yates;

FLETCHER, PAUL

Bolton-born forward Paul Fletcher began his league career with his home-town club and in 42 games for the then Burnden Park club,

scored seven goals before his £60,000 move to Burnley in March 1971. After making his debut in a 1-0 home defeat by Southampton, Fletcher settled into the Burnley side, forming a fine striking partnership with Frank Casper. In 1972-73, Fletcher topped the club's scoring charts as they won the Second Division Championship. His total of 15 goals included a hat-trick in a 3-0 home win over Cardiff City. He headed the scoring lists again in 1973-74 as the Clarets finished sixth in Division One. That season, Burnley reached the final of the

Paul Fletcher, scorer of one of the most talked-about goals by a Burnley player.

Texaco Cup with Fletcher netting a hat-trick in a 7-0 win over East Fife in round one. Fletcher went on to score 86 goals in 352 games for the Clarets with his acrobatic overhead bicycle-kick goal against Leeds United still talked about by Burnley fans.

On leaving Turf Moor, he joined Blackpool but after an injury-ravaged spell at Bloomfield Road, he hung up his boots. After working as commercial manager for Colne Dynamoes, he took up a similar role with Huddersfield Town before becoming the Yorkshire club's chief executive. He later returned to his first club in that capacity at their new Reebok Stadium.

FLOODLIGHTS

Floodlights were installed at Turf Moor in 1957 and first switched on for a friendly match against Blackburn Rovers on 16 December 1957. They were replaced in 1975 by new ones costing in the region of £30,000 and first used in February of that year for a Lancashire schoolboys match.

FLYNN, BRIAN

A Welsh Schoolboy international, Brian Flynn joined the Clarets as an apprentice in 1971, making his league debut in a 1-1 draw at Arsenal in February 1974. It was midway through the following season that Flynn began to establish himself in the Burnley side, his form leading to him winning the first of 66 Welsh caps at the age of 19 in a win over Luxembourg at the Vetch Field. In November 1977, Flynn left Turf Moor, joining Leeds United for £175,000.

His midfield partnership with Tony Currie was the best of the post-Revie era where his neat control, hard work and passing ability put him among the best midfielders of his day. He had appeared in 177 League and Cup games for the Elland Road club when he returned to Turf Moor on loan. Eight months later in November 1982 he joined Burnley on a permanent basis, the move costing the Clarets £60,000. He took his tally of goals to 27 in 253 games before then playing for Cardiff City, Doncaster Rovers and Bury. After coaching Limerick, he had another spell at Belle Vue before returning to Turf Moor as the club's Football in the Community Officer. He later joined Wrexham, taking over the player-manager's role from Dixie McNeill early in the 1989-90 season. After hanging up his boots to concentrate solely on management, he saw the Robins finish bottom of the Fourth Division in 1990-91 before leading the club to promotion to the 'new' Second Division in 1992-93. Since then the club have been close to the play-offs on a number of occasions, perhaps none more so than in 1997-98 when they finished seventh.

FOOTBALLER OF THE YEAR

The Football Writers' Association Footballer of the Year award has been won by a Burnley player on just one occasion and that was by Jimmy Adamson in 1961-62.

FOOTBALL LEAGUE CUP

The club first took part in the inaugural competition in 1960-61 when they reached the semi-final. In their first match, a Gordon Harris hat-trick helped them beat Cardiff City 4-0 before wins against Brentford (Home 2-1 after a 1-1 draw) Nottingham Forest (Home 2-1) and Southampton (Away 4-2) paired them with Aston Villa in the two-legged semi-final. Following a 1-1 draw at Turf Moor and a 2-2 draw at Villa Park, the two clubs met in a third match at Old Trafford which Villa won 2-1. The Clarets did not enter the competition for the next four seasons but when they rejoined in 1965-66, Andy Lochhead netted a hat-trick in their first match as Doncaster Rovers were beaten 4-0. The Clarets progressed to the fifth round where they went out of the competition to Peterborough United by the same scoreline.

The club reached the semi-finals for a second time in 1968-69, beating Grimsby Town (Home 6-0 after a 1-1 draw) Workington (Away 1-0) Leicester City (Home 4-0) and Crystal Palace (Home 2-0). In the semi-finals Burnley met Swindon Town and once again the tie necessitated a third match after both club's had won their away leg 2-1. In the replay a late goal by future Claret Peter Noble deep into extra-time gave the Wiltshire club a 3-2 win and a place in the final.

Burnley reached the semi-final stage for a third time in 1982-83. After beating Bury 8-4 on aggregate in the first round, the Clarets disposed of Middlesborough 4-3, again over two legs before going on to victories over Coventry City (Away 2-1) Birmingham City (Home 3-2) and Tottenham Hotspur (Away 4-1). The club's opponents in the semi-final were Liverpool but after losing the first leg at Anfield 3-0, the Clarets failed to reach the Wembley final despite winning the return 1-0, courtesy of a Derek Scott goal.

FOOTBALL LEAGUE GROUP CUP

The Football League Group Cup was founded in 1981 as a replacement to the defunct Anglo-Scottish Cup. Burnley were one of 32 entrants invited from those Second, Third and Fourth Division clubs who had shown an interest in participating in the competition. The clubs were divided into eight groups of four with the top team from each group playing in a knock-out stage later in the season.

The Clarets topped their group, beating Carlisle United (Home 4-2) and Preston North End (Away 1-0) and drawing 0-0 at Blackpool. In the quarter-final, goals from Scott and Holt gave Burnley a 2-1 home win over Watford but then they crashed 5-1 at Wimbledon in the semi-final stage of the competition.

FOUNDATION

The majority of people responsible for the formation of the Burnley club in 1881 were from the defunct rugby club, Burnley Rovers. In fact, they continued to play rugby for a year before changing to soccer and dropping 'Rovers' from their name. The changes were decided at a meeting held in May 1882 at the Bull Hotel.

FOURTH DIVISION

The Clarets have had just one spell in the Fourth Division. Following their relegation in 1984-85, the club spent seven seasons in the League's basement. Burnley won their first-ever Division Four game, beating Northampton Town 3-2 but in October 1965, manager Martin Buchan resigned. He was replaced by Tommy Cavanagh who led the Clarets to a disappointing 14th position. He was replaced by Briam Miler for the start of the 1986-87 season but by the time the final game of the season against Orient came round, Burnley needed to win to avoid relegation to the Vauxhall Conference. Goals from Grewcock and Britton helped the Clarets to a 2-1 win, whilst Lincoln City lost their last game and their Football League status. There followed three seasons of mid-table placings before the club finished sixth in 1990-91 to qualify for the end of season play-offs. Unfortunately the club lost 2-1 over two legs to Torquay United. The Clarets won the Fourth Division Championship the following season with 83 points, the club's best points tally.

FRANCIS, JOHN

After playing his early football for Halifax Town, winger John Francis joined non-League Emley and appeared for the Yorkshire side in the 1988 FA Vase Final against Colne Dynamoes. In the close season he joined Sheffield United and was a member of the Blades' side that won successive promotions from the Third to the First Division.

He joined Burnley in January 1990 for a fee of £90,000 and made his debut the following month in a 2-1 home defeat by Gillingham. In his first full season at Turf Moor, he helped the Clarets reach the Fourth Division play-offs whilst in 1991-92 his electrifying pace was instrumental in the club's success in winning the Fourth Division Championship. At the end of the season he was sold to Cambridge United but returned to Turf Moor after less than a season with the East Anglian club. His second spell with Burnley was blighted by a knee injury and after taking his tally of goals to 49 in 236 games, he joined Scunthorpe United as a non-contract player. Still unable to get back to his speedy best, he left to play non-League football for Halifax Town.

FREEMAN, BERT

Bert Freeman was a footballing legend at the turn of the century, having started his career with Birmingham youth sides, Gower Old Boys and Aston Manor before signing for Aston Villa in April 1904. Unable to break into Villa's first team, he joined Woolwich Arsenal and made a goalscoring debut at Nottingham Forest. He ended his first season with 12 goals in 21 games and helped the Gunners to their first-ever FA Cup semi-final. In April 1908 he left to join Everton and the following season created a new First Division record when he scored 38 goals in 37 games. He scored two against Woolwich Arsenal in the opening game of the season and went on to net hat-tricks against Sheffield United (Away 5-1); Sunderland (Home 4-0); Sheffield United (Home 5-1); and Chelsea (Home 3-2). He topped the club's scoring charts again in 1909-10 with 22 goals in the league and a further four in FA Cup games including hat-tricks against Sheffield Wednesday (Away 3-1) and Bolton Wanderers (Home 3-1). After playing in the North v South England trial at Fulham, he won two full caps against Wales and Scotland as well as scoring four goals for the Football League against the Irish League. After three seasons at Goodison Park in which he scored 67 goals in 94 games, he was surprisingly allowed to leave and join Burnley.

In 1911-12, Freeman scored 32 goals in 33 League games including hat-tricks against Fulham (Away 4-3) Glossop (Home 4-0) and Fulham (Home 5-1) to top the Football League's scoring charts. He repeated the feat the following season as the club won promotion to the First Division, his total of 31 goals in 37 games including another hat-trick in a 5-1 home win over Leicester Fosse. He was still the club's leading scorer in 1913-14, netting his fifth hat-trick in a 5-1 defeat of Derby County but more importantly, scoring the only goal of the FA Cup Final as the Clarets beat Liverpool 1-0. Unfortunately he lost four good years to the First World War but was still the club's first-choice centre-forward when League football resumed in 1919-20. He took his tally of goals to 115 in 189 games before leaving to play for Wigan Borough and later Kettering.

FREIGHT ROVER TROPHY

A competition designed solely and specifically for the Associate Members of the Football League, the Freight Rover Trophy replaced the initial Associate Members Cup for the 1984-85 season. Burnley's first game in the competition saw them beat Stockport County 5-1 with Wayne Biggins netting two of the goals. In the return leg at Edgeley Park, Kevin Hird scored the only goal of the game to give the Clarets an aggregate win of 6-1. In the second round, Burnley drew 2-2 at Tranmere Rovers but lost 5-4 on the resultant penalty shoot-out. Still qualifying for the third round, the Clarets drew 1-1 at Mansfield Town before again losing on penalties.

In 1985-86 Burnley beat Chesterfield 2-1 and drew 1-1 with Darlington with Alan Taylor scoring in both matches but it wasn't enough to take them through to the knockout stages of the competition.

After beating Blackpool 3-2 in the opening group game in 1986-87, the Clarets lost 2-0 at home to Bolton Wanderers but still qualified for the knockout stages. The first round tie saw Burnley travel to Burnden Park to play Bolton again but despite an early goal by Parker, the Clarets lost 2-1.

GOALKEEPERS

Burnley FC has almost always been extremely well served by its goalkeepers and most of them have been highly popular with the supporters.

Jack Hillman was Burnley's first 'keeper of note, making 188 League and Cup appearances in two spells with the club. An England international, he was banned for a complete season in 1900-01 after being found guilty of trying to bribe Nottingham Forest players before the final match of the previous season. Billy Green made an immediate impact at Turf Moor following his transfer from Brentford in 1903, going on to play in 153 first team games. He was replaced by Jerry Dawson, who after making his debut in a 3-0 home win over Stockport County in April 1907, went on to play in 569 League and Cup games, a club record. Dawson won two full caps for England and was instrumental in the club winning the League Championship in 1920-21. Jimmy Strong played in 203 consecutive league games following his debut in a 1-1 draw at Coventry on the opening day of the 1946-47 season. He was the club's first-choice 'keeper until being replaced by Colin McDonald, the son of a former Football League goalkeeper. McDonald played in all of England's 1958 World Cup matches and was voted the tournaments best 'keeper. Sadly his career was brought to a premature end when he broke his leg whilst representing the Football League in Dublin. It was Adam Blacklaw who benefited from McDonald's retirement, his performances in the club's League Championship winning season of 1959-60 earning him international recognition for Scotland. Harry Thomson not only saved a penalty on his debut at Leicester City but in February 1967 played the game of his life in a goalless draw at Naples, making another penalty save! Alan Stevenson was the club's first-choice 'keeper for 12 seasons, helping the Clarets win both the Second and Third Division Championships but was surprisingly allowed to leave Turf Moor when he was just two games short of establishing a new post-war appearance record for the club. Marlon Beresford, who joined Burnley from Sheffield Wednesday in the summer of 1992 went on to prove himself to be one of the best 'keepers outside of the Premier League. He had appeared in 294 games for the Clarets when Middlesborough paid £500,000 for his services in March 1998.

GOALS

The most goals Burnley have ever scored in one game is nine. The club have won four games by a 9-0 scoreline – Darwen (1891-92); Crystal Palace (1908-09); New Brighton (1956-57); and Penrith

(1984-85). The only other time that the club have scored nine goals was in 1897-98 when they beat Loughborough 9-3.

GOALS – CAREER BEST

The highest goalscorer in the club's history is George Beel, who between seasons 1923-24 and 1931-32, netted 187 goals for the club. These comprised 178 in the League and nine in the FA Cup.

GOALS – INDIVIDUAL

Louis Page scored six of Burnley's goals on 10 Aril 1926 when they beat Birmingham 7-1 at St Andrew's. There are five Burnley players who have scored five goals in a game for the club, with Andy Lochhead achieving the feat on two occasions. The first player to score five goals was Jimmy Ross on 28 March 1898 in a 9-0 home win over Loughborough Town. Joe Anderson was the next Clarets' player to score five in a 7-1 win over Aston Villa on 5 February 1921. When Burnley beat Nottingham Forest 8-0 on 21 November 1959, Jimmy Robson scored five of the club's goals. Andy Lochhead achieved the feat on 24 April 1965 as Chelsea were beaten 6-2 and again on 25 January 1966 in a 7-0 FA Cup win over Bournemouth. The last Burnley player to score five goals is Paul Barnes who scored all five goals on 5 October 1996 as the Clarets beat Stockport County 5-2.

GOALS – SEASON

The club's highest league goalscorer in any one season remains George Beel who scored 35 league goals in 1927-28 as the Clarets finished 19th in the First Division. Jimmy Robson and Willie Irvine hold the club record for the season's highest tally in all matches with 37 goals, scored in seasons 1960-61 and 1965-66 respectively.

GOALSCORING RECORDS

George Beel holds a number of club goalscoring records. He has scored the most goals in the Football League with a total of 178, holds the record for the most goals in a season with 35 in 1927-28 and has netted a record 11 hat-tricks.

GRAY, BILLY

Joining Leyton Orient from Dinnington Colliery, the Durham-born winger soon attracted the attention of the bigger clubs and was snapped up by Chelsea in March 1949. He spent four years at Stamford Bridge, scoring 12 goals in his 146 League appearances and winning an England 'B' cap before signing for Burnley in June 1953 for £16,000.

He made his debut in a 4-1 home win over Wolves on the opening day of the 1953-54 season, scoring six goals in his first seven games. He ended the campaign as the club's leading scorer with 19 goals including hat-tricks against Tottenham Hotspur (Home 4-2) and Middlesborough (Home 5-0).

Gray was a virtual ever-present in the Clarets' side until he joined Nottingham Forest in the summer of 1957, having scored 32 goals in 130 games.

The City Ground club converted the winger into a scheming inside-forward and later to full-back as they sought to get the best out of the former Burnley player. He won a FA Cup winners' medal in 1959 and went on to appear in 223 games for Forest before joining Millwall as player-manager. Though the Lions were relegated to the Fourth Division, within two years he had reversed their fortunes and they were back in the Second Division. He later managed Brentford and Notts County before returning to the City Ground as Forest's groundsman.

GREWCOCK, NEIL

Neil Grewcock began his career with his home-town club Leicester City before moving to Gillingham after just eight league appearances for the Foxes. The Priestfield Stadium club released him in the summer of 1983 and he moved into non-League football with Shepshed Charterhouse. He joined Burnley in June 1984 and made his debut in a 1-1 home draw against Plymouth Argyle on the opening day of the 1984-85 season.

Grewcock was extremely popular with the Burnley fans, not only for his exciting wing play and pin-point crosses but also for the spectacular goals he scored. However, without doubt the most important goal Grewcock scored came on 9 May 1987 as Burnley beat Orient 2-1 to secure their Football League status.

During the club's run to the Sherpa Van Trophy Final, Grewcock was injured in the Northern Area semi-final against Halifax Town and was out of the game for over a year. He returned to help the Clarets to the Fourth Division play-offs in 1991 but was released at the end of the season after scoring 35 goals in 255 games.

GUEST PLAYERS

The guest system was used by all clubs during both world wars. Although on occasions it was abused almost beyond belief (some sides that opposed Burnley had ten or eleven guests!) it normally worked sensibly and effectively and to the benefit of players, clubs and supporters. During the Second World War, Burnley had the services of five top-class goalkeepers in Ted Sagar (Everton) Harry Holdcroft (Preston North End) Jimmy Strong (Walsall) Jack Fairbrother (Preston North End and later Newcastle United) and Cyril Sidlow (Wolverhampton Wanderers and later Liverpool) who had already won 11 wartime caps.

A number of Burnley players also 'guested' for other clubs. These included John Billingham (Northampton Town) Ronnie Hornby (Rochdale and Bury) Jack Knight (Bolton Wanderers) Len Martindale (Bolton Wanderers) and Harry Potts (Fulham, Bury and Sunderland).

H

HAMILTON, BILLY

After beginning his football career with Linfield, Billy Hamilton joined Queen's Park Rangers but was unable to settle at Loftus Road and in November 1979 he was transferred to Burnley for £38,000. After making his debut in a goalless draw at Bristol Rovers, Hamilton scored his first goal for the club in the famous 3-2 win over Newcastle United on Boxing Day. He soon formed a prolific goalscoring partnership with Steve Taylor and in 1981-82 he top scored as the Clarets won the Third Division Championship. He also netted his first hat-trick for the club in a 6-0 FA Cup third round win over non-League Altrincham. Though the club were relegated the following season, Hamilton was the leading scorer with 12 goals, his total including hat-tricks in the wins over Carlisle United (Home 4-1) and

Billy Hamilton, Northern Ireland international who top scored during the Third Division Championship winning season of 1881-82.

Charlton Athletic (Home 7-1). He netted another hat-trick in 1983-84 as Bournemouth were beaten 5-1 but at the end of the season, the Northern Ireland international who had taken his total of goals to 77 in 252 games, joined Oxford United.

Forming a fine partnership with John Aldridge, he helped the Manor Ground club reach the First Division before he was forced to retire through injury. He later became player-manager of Limerick before holding a similar position with Distillery.

HANKIN, RAY

An England Youth international, Ray Hankin made his Burnley debut as a substitute for Frank Casper in a 3-0 home win over Luton Town in April 1973. In the close season he played in the England youth side that won the Little World Cup in Italy, scoring one of England's goals in a 3-2 win over East Germany in the final.

He established himself in the Burnley side in 1973-74 playing alongside Paul Fletcher. His form led to him winning selection for the England Under-23 side but in September 1976 after scoring 46 goals in 138 games he was transferred to Leeds United for £172,000.

Injury restricted his appearances in his first season at Elland Road before he came back as a fearsome spearhead the following season, when he topped 20 league goals. In March 1980 he joined Vancouver Whitecaps and won an NASL north-west Division winners' medal in 1981. In November of that year, Arsenal were prepared to pay £400,000 for his scoring talents but although he signed on a trial basis, he was released without a senior appearance. After a brief spell as Shamrock Rovers he returned to Vancouver, then joined Middlesborough. He later played for Peterborough United, Wolves, Whitby Town and Guisborough Town. He was appointed manager of Northallerton Town in March 1989 but now works as Newcastle United's Football in the Community Officer.

HARRIS, GORDON

Gordon 'Bomber' Harris was working down the pit and representing his colliery at Firbeck when Burnley signed him in January 1958. He made his first team debut some 12 months later, scoring for the Clarets in a 3-1 home win over Leeds United. However, it was 1960-61 before he established himself as a first team regular, scoring 14 goals in 31 games including a hat-trick in a 4-0 League Cup win at Cardiff City. The following season was Harris' best in terms of goals scored, the Worksop-born forward netting 17 times. He also appeared in the Burnley side that lost 3-1 to Spurs in the FA Cup Final. His form led to him winning his first representative honours when in November 1961 he played for the Football League against the Irish League. A week later he represented the England Under-23s against Israel at Elland Road. In January 1966, Harris won his only full cap when he played in the 1-1 draw against Poland at Goodison Park. He was appointed Burnley captain for the 1967-68 season but just before Christmas he was dropped and disciplined following differences of opinion with other players during training!

Shortly afterwards, Harris, who had scored 81 goals in 313 games including another hat-trick in a 4-0 win over Sheffield United on the opening day of the 1966-67 season, joined Sunderland.

He scored 16 goals in 136 outings for the Wearsiders before retiring from league football and seeing out his career with non-League South Shields.

HAT-TRICKS

Claude Lambie scored Burnley's first hat-trick in the Football League in the Clarets' 7-0 home win over Bolton Wanderers on 1 March 1890.

Louis Page is the only Burnley player to score a double hat-trick in a senior match for the club. On 10 April 1926, the flying winger was tried at centre-forward for Burnley's match at Birmingham City. The change in position proved a great success as he scored six of the club's goals in a 7-1 win.

Tom Nicol scored a hat-trick on his debut in a 6-2 win over Preston North End on 7 March 1891.

Ian Lawson scored four goals for Burnley on his first team debut on 5 January 1957 as Chesterfield were beaten 7-0 in a FA Cup third round tie.

Jimmy Robson, who was the club's top scorer in 1960-61. netted three hat-tricks in the space of seven games early in the season – Preston North End (Home 4-2) Fulham (Home 5-0) and Chelsea (Away 6-2). Willie Irvine also scored three hat-tricks in 1965-66 as the club finished third in Division One. His trebles were against Northampton Town (Home 4-1) Fulham (Away 5-2) and Nottingham Forest (Home 4-1).

George Beel holds the club record for the most hat-tricks for the club with a total of 11.

HAWORTH, JOHN

John Haworth played right-back for Meadow Bank FC before becoming the club's secretary. In 1897 he joined Accrington Stanley as a committee member and later in the year became that club's secretary. With Haworth as secretary, Accrington Stanley won the Lancashire Combination in 1902-03 and 1905-06 before leaving to become Burnley's secretary-manager in 1910. Haworth employed Charlie Bates as his trainer and decided to change the club's colours from green to the claret and blue of the current League Champions Aston Villa.

Towards the end of his first season in charge, Haworth signed the Everton centre-forward Bert Freeman and early the following season, Barnsley's Tommy Boyle.

In 1912-13 the club gained promotion to the First Division and a FA Cup semi-final was also reached. The FA Cup was won in 1914 when Liverpool were beaten 1-0 in the final at Crystal Palace. The Clarets finished runners-up in the First Division in 1919-20 before walking away with the Championship the following season, finishing five points clear of Manchester City. The club were third in 1921-22 but the club's successful days were coming to an end. In 1924, John Haworth caught pneumonia and died whilst still in office.

HEATH, ADRIAN

Starting his career with his home-town club Stoke City, Adrian Heath appeared briefly during the Potters' Second Division promotion-winning season of 1978-79. He became a virtual fixture in the club's midfield the following season where his performances led to him winning England Under-21 honours. In January 1982 Heath joined Everton for a Goodison Park record fee of £700,000. He was the

club's top scorer in 1983-84 with 18 goals and won an FA Cup winners' medal as Everton beat Watford 2-0. In 1986-87 the Goodison club won the League Championship with Heath an influential member of the side. After scoring 89 goals in 293 games, Heath joined Spanish club, Espanol but after less than a season, returned to play for Aston Villa. In February 1990 he signed for Manchester City, once more linking up with Howard Kendall. He returned to Stoke in March 1992 but five months later, he joined Burnley.

Adrian Heath who, in 1992-93, scored 20 goals, the best of his career.

His first season at Turf Moor saw him score 20 goals in 43 league games, the best of his career. After the club were relegated, he accepted the position of assistant-manager at Sheffield United but returned to Turf Moor in February 1996 as the new Burnley manager when Jimmy Mullen was relieved of his duties.

A highly skilled technician, he took his total of appearances in which he scored 35 goals to 148 before hanging up his boots to concentrate fully on management. Yet' in June 1997' he resigned his post to rejoin Howard Kendall's Everton as first team coach. Heath is now manager of Sheffield United.

HILL, FRANK

Frank Hill began his career with Forfar Athletic before joining Aberdeen in the summer of 1928. With the Dons he won three Scottish caps and represented the Scottish League. Nicknamed 'Tiger' because of his ferocious tackling, he was transferred to Arsenal for £3,000 in May 1932. During his four seasons at Highbury, he won three League Championship medals but after appearing in 83 first team games, he left to play for Blackpool. Appointed captain, he helped the Seasiders win promotion before moving to Southampton where he played in the two seasons leading up to the Second World War.

During the war he became assistant-trainer to Preston North End and was a flight lieutenant in India with the RAF. Hill later became player-manager of Crewe Alexandra before becoming Burnley manager in September 1948.

In his six seasons in charge at Turf Moor, the Clarets played some attractive football and had a best finish of sixth in the First Division in 1952-53. He had a reputation for being shrewd in the transfer market, the prime example being the acquisition of Jimmy McIlroy from Glentoran for £7,000.

Hill left Turf Moor in 1954 to manage Preston North End before becoming a coach in Iraq. He returned to England to take charge of Notts County, guiding them to promotion from the Third Division in 1959-60. He later managed Charlton Athletic before scouting for Manchester City.

HILL, JAMES

Able to play in any forward position, James Hill joined the Clarets from St Mirren in December 1889 and made his debut in a 3-1 defeat at Stoke early the following year. When he arrived at Turf Moor the club were lying at the bottom of the League and it was his partnership with Claude Lambie that helped them win four of its last five matches and so retain their top flight status.

The club's first real consistent goalscorer, Hill's best season was 1893-94 when he netted 11 goals in 25 games but his only hat-trick for the club came two seasons later in a 4-3 win at Bury. Hill went on to score 41 goals in 162 games for the Clarets before leaving Turf Moor in January 1897 to play for Stoke.

He had one and a half seasons at the Victoria Ground before like a number of players he was tempted to sign for New Brighton Tower who were offering higher money as they sought out a team to fit their lofty ambitions.

HILLMAN, JACK

Goalkeeper Jack Hillman was second only to the huge Sheffield United 'keeper Billy Foulke in stature, standing over 6 feet tall and weighing 16 stone. He was a Devon man, born at Tavistock but after moving to Burnley as a child, it was with the Turf Moor club that he began his career.

He made his debut in a 1-0 defeat at Accrington on the opening day of the 1891-92 season, a campaign in which he was ever-present. After four seasons with the Clarets, he joined Everton, playing in 38 games before signing for Dundee. His stay in Scotland was short and in March 1898 he returned to Turf Moor.

The following season he made his full international debut for England in the 13-2 win over Ireland at Sunderland. This larger than life character was banned for the entire 1900-01 season following an attempt to bribe Nottingham Forest players to 'throw' the last game of the 1899-1900 season and so enable Burnley to avoid relegation to the Second Division. He returned to the Clarets' side the following season, taking his total of first team appearances to 188 before joining Manchester City.

He helped them win the Second Division Championship in 1903 and the FA Cup Final in 1904. He later played for Millwall before returning to Turf Moor again, this time as the club's trainer.

HODGSON, TEDDY

Chorley-born inside-forward Teddy Hodgson played his first game for the Clarets in a 1-1 draw at Barnsley in September 1911, going on to score seven goals in 20 games as the club finished third in Division Two. Included in his total was his first hat-trick for the club in a 4-1 home win over Stockport County. In 1912-13 Burnley won promotion to the First Division with Hodgson scoring 15 goals in 32 games.

The following season, Hodgson's partnership with Bert Freeman began to flourish and helped the club win the FA Cup. On their way to the final, Hodgson, who was the club's leading scorer in that Cup run, netted a hat-trick in a 3-2 win over Derby County. Earlier in the league season, he had hit another treble in a 6-1 home win over Chelsea. His best season in terms of goals scored was 1914-15 when he topped the club's scoring charts with 20 goals in 39 games as the Clarets finished fourth in Division One.

Hodgson, who had scored 62 goals in 137 games, joined the Army in 1916 and, when the First World War ended, was in Germany. He had been badly wounded but on being transferred to hospital in England, his condition deteriorated and he sadly died at the age of only 33.

HOLDEN, BILLY

After spending his National Service in the Military Police, Bill Holden worked for a Radcliffe company where he was spotted playing for the works team. After an unsuccessful trial with Everton, he was recommended to Burnley, who signed him in November 1949.

From the time he made his debut in a 3-1 home win over Middlesborough in September 1950, he was the Clarets' regular centre-forward for the next five years. During his period at Turf Moor, Holden played for England 'B' against Scotland in 1953.

Holden was the club's leading scorer in 1950-51, 1952-53 and 1954-55 with his best return being his 24 League and Cup goals in 1952-53. That season, Holden scored four goals in a 5-1 home win over Sunderland, having netted his first hat-trick for the club in a 7-1 defeat of Middlesborough in December 1951. Holden's last hat-trick was in the 5-2 win at Arsenal in October 1953. He had scored 79 goals in 199 games when he left Turf Moor to join Sunderland for £12,000. He made his debut at St James Park and though he scored after four minutes, Newcastle United won the 1955 Boxing Day encounter. Following a dispute with the management, he was transfer listed and after just 19 appearances, he joined Stockport County for a bargain £6,000.He was the club's top scorer in 1957-58 but after finding the net 40 times in 96 games he moved to Bury before ending his career with Halifax Town

HOME MATCHES

The club's best home win in the Football League is 9-0 against Darwen on 9 January 1892. The Clarets have repeated the scoreline in two FA Cup matches against Crystal Palace in 1908-09 and New Brighton in 1956-57. Burnley also scored nine goals at home to Loughborough on 28 March 1898, winning 9-3. Burnley have scored eight goals at home in a match on three occasions. They beat Nottingham Forest 8-2 on 4 November 1922; Reading 8-1 on 13 September 1930 and Nottingham Forest again 8-0 on 21 November 1959.

The club's worst home defeat is 7-1, a scoreline inflicted on the club by Blackburn Rovers in 1888-89 and Arsenal in the 1936-37 FA Cup competition.

HOME SEASONS

Burnley have gone through a complete league season without losing a single home game on three occasions – 1897-98, 1900-01 and 1911-12 – winning the Second Division Championship in 1897-98 and finishing third in Division Two on the other two occasions. The club's highest number of home wins in a league season is 17, a figure achieved in seasons 1920-21, 1990-91 and 1993-94.

HONOURS

The major honours achieved by the club are:

First Division Championship	1920-21	1959-60
Runners-Up	1919-20	1961-62
Second Division Championship	1897-98	1972-73
Runners-Up	1912-13	1946-47
Third Division Championship	1981-82	
Fourth Division Championship	1991-92	
FA Cup Winners	1914	
Runners-Up	1947	1962
Anglo-Scottish Cup Winners	1979	
Texaco Cup Winners	1974	
Sherpa Van Trophy Runners-Up	1988	
FA Youth Cup Winners	1968	

HUNDRED GOALS

Burnley have scored more than 100 league goals in a season on two occasions. The club's highest total is 102 goals scored in 1960-61, when they came fourth in Division One. The following season the Clarets scored 101 goals when finishing runners-up to Ipswich Town in the First Division.

INGHAM, BILLY

Utility player Billy Ingham played his first game for the club as a substitute for Alan West in a 2-0 home defeat by Hull City in February 1972. When the Clarets won the Second Division Championship in 1972-73, Ingham played in 18 games, seven as a substitute and scored four goals. He was an important member of the Burnley squad for seven seasons, making 265 appearances both at full-back and in midfield and scoring 31 goals.

Ingham left Turf Moor in August 1980 to play for Bradford City for a fee of £30,000 but is stay at Valley Parade was brief and though he helped them win promotion from the Fourth Division in 1981-82, he wasn't retained. He then played non-League football for Accrington Stanley before hanging up his boots.

INTER-CITIES FAIRS CUP

In 1966-67 the Clarets reached the quarter-finals of the Inter Cities Fairs Cup. After beating Stuttgart 3-1 on aggregate in the first round, Burnley were drawn against Swiss side Lausanne in round two. The Turf Moor side played some magnificent football to win through to round three with an excellent 8-1 aggregate win. Andy Lochhead who had scored one of Burnley's goals in Switzerland, netted a second-leg hat-trick as the Clarets won the Turf Moor leg 5-0. The third round tie against Italian giants Napoli is remembered more for its violence on the field which saw Panzanato sent-off and both captains warned as to the conduct of their players, rather than Burnley's 3-0 victory at Turf Moor and the goalless draw they played out in the away leg.

In the quarter-final, the club were drawn away to Eintrackt Frankfurt. After a Brian Miller goal had given them a 1-1 draw in Germany, much was hoped for in the second leg. But despite numerous chances, the visitors' defence held firm and by the time Miller scored his second goal of the tie, the Clarets were already 2-0 down on the night and on their way out of the competition.

INTERNATIONAL PLAYERS

Burnley's most capped player (i.e. caps gained while players were registered with the club) is Jimmy McIlroy with 51 caps. The following is a complete list of players who have gained full international honours while at Turf Moor.

England	Caps	Scotland	Caps
John Angus	1	Jock Aird	4
William Bannister	1	Adam Blacklaw	3
Tommy Boyle	1	Willie Morgan	1
Jack Bruton	3	**Wales**	
Ralph Coates	2	Stan Bowsher	1
John Connelly	10	Brian Flynn	33
James Crabtree	3	Leighton James	22
Jerry Dawson	2	Billy Morris	5
Martin Dobson	4	**Northern Ireland**	
Billy Elliott	5	Tommy Cassidy	4
Bert Freeman	3	Terry Cochrane	4
Gordon Harris	1	Alex Elder	34
Jack Hill	8	William Emerson	5
Jack Hillman	1	Hugh Flack	1
Bob Kelly	11	Billy Hamilton	34
Colin McDonald	8	Willie Irvine	17
Brian Miller	1	Andy McCluggage	11
Eddie Moscrop	2	Jimmy McIlroy	51
Louis Page	7	Tom Morrison	4
Brian Pilkington	1	Sammy Todd	8
Ray Pointer	3	Tom Willighan	2
George Waterfield	1		
Billy Watson	3		
Jack Yates	1		

Burnley's first player to be capped was James Crabtree who played for England v Ireland at Belfast in 1894.

Willie Irvine, Northern Ireland international who scored a hat-trick on his Burnley home debut.

IRVINE, WILLIE

One of the game's most prolific goalscorers, Willie Irvine scored on his debut on 11 May 1963 as the Clarets won 3-2 at Arsenal. Three days later in the final game of the season, Irvine netted a hat-trick on his home debut as Burnley beat Birmingham City 3-1. Despite this early success, the form of Lochhead and Robson kept Irvine out of the first team until 1964-65 when he formed a deadly striking partnership with Andy Lochhead. Irvine scored 21 goals in 38 games including a hat-trick in a 4-0 home win over Fulham. In 1965-66 he topped the club's scoring charts with 29 goals including hat-tricks in the victories over Northampton Town (Home 4-1) Fulham (Away 5-2) and Nottingham Forest (Home 4-1). Midway through the following season, the Northern Ireland international broke his leg in an FA Cup third round replay at Everton and though he recovered to take his tally of goals to 97 in 148 games, he was never really the same player again.

In March 1968 he joined Preston North End for £45,000 and as with Burnley, he scored on his debut before netting a hat-trick on his home debut in a 3-1 win over Huddersfield Town. Though the Deepdale club were struggling, Irvine continued to find the net and in 1971 joined Brighton and Hove Albion. He helped the Seagulls win promotion to the Second Division before ending his league career with Halifax Town.

J

JAKUB, JOE

Of Polish ancestry, Joe Jakub joined the Turf Moor club as an apprentice in December 1973, eventually making his debut in a 3-1 home defeat by Coventry City on the final day of the 1975-76 season.

However, the versatile Jakub found it difficult to establish himself in the first team and only made six league appearances over the next three seasons. In October 1980 he left the Clarets to play for Bury.

In six years with the Shakers he appeared in 265 league games and captained the club to the Third Division Championship in 1984-85. Midway through the 1986-87 season he went to play for AZ67 Alkmaar, returning to play for Chester City in August 1988. After just one season at Sealand Road, Jakub returned to play for Burnley and took his tally of goals to nine in 269 games.

Following his release at the end of the 1992-93 campaign, he returned to Chester for one more season before joining Wigan Athletic

Joe Jakub, seen here in his Wigan Athletic days

where he ended his playing days. He remained in the game, joining the coaching staff of Preston North End.

JAMES, LEIGHTON

Another outstanding product of the Burnley youth scheme, Leighton James played his first game for the club in a 2-1 home win over Nottingham Forest during the club's relegation season of 1970-71. Primarily a right-footed player, he played most of his games on the left-wing. Like many other wingers, he often felt that he didn't receive the protection he deserved and was occasionally seen complaining to the referee about the treatment he was receiving from the opposition!

At times, Leighton James was brilliant – a player of undeniable pace and skill. As well as setting up chances for others, he was quite capable of scoring goals and spectacular ones at that. He would cut in from the left flank and shoot with his favourite right foot – it was a great asset. James could drive the ball or curl it, the accuracy of his shooting also earning him a reputation as one of the game's best free-kick specialists. His best years were at Turf Moor where he emerged alongside other Burnley youth team products like Ralph Coates, Martin Dobson and Dave Thomas. Unfortunately for Burnley,. James like the other three had to be sold to help balance the club's books. In November 1975 he joined Derby County for £310,000 but after two seasons at the Baseball Ground in which he never really settled, he moved to Queen's Park Rangers. But within a year he was back at Turf Moor.

He was by now an established Welsh international, having made his debut in the 1971-72 season and he went on to score 10 goals in 54 appearances for his country. A competent and shrewd player, you probably wouldn't have guessed that he was a professional footballer. For he wore glasses and had a very mild manner – yet on the field of play, he knew all the tricks!

Leighton James – Welsh international who, in three spells with the Clarets, scored 81 goals in 403 games.

In 1980 his Welsh team-mate John Toshack signed him for Swansea City. Playing in his native country, James was a major influence in helping the Swans reach the First Division for the first time in the club's history. He later played for Sunderland, Bury and Newport County before rejoining Burnley as player-coach in the summer of 1986. He took his tally of goals for the club to 81 in 403 appearances before becoming Bradford City's coach. After spells in management with Gainsborough Trinity and Morecambe, he can now be heard n local radio's sports programmes.

K

KELLY, BOB

Bob Kelly was first spotted when playing for St Helen's Town, where his performances attracted the attention of a number of top clubs. It was newly-promoted Burnley who won the race for his signature when they paid £300 for his services in November 1913. He scored on his debut as the Clarets beat Aston Villa 4-0 but he only made seven league appearances that season, failing to win a place in the club's FA Cup winning side. The following season he won a regular place in the Burnley side, forming a good partnership with Bert Freeman and scoring 10 goals in 27 games.

In the first season of League football following the hostilities, Kelly was at his best, helping the club to finish runners-up in the First Division. His form that season led to him winning the first of 14 full caps for England when he scored twice in a 5-4 win over Scotland at Sheffield.

In 1920-21, Bob Kelly was an influential member of Burnley's League Championship winning side, scoring 20 goals in 37 games including four in a 7-1 home win over Oldham Athletic. He continued to score on a regular basis for the Clarets and in December 1921 netted his second hat-trick for the club in a 3-1 defeat of Middlesborough. He went on to score 97 goals in 299 League and Cup games before leaving Turf Moor in December 1925 to join Sunderland for £6,500.

He scored 14 goals in 55 games for the Wearsiders before signing for Huddersfield Town. After more than 200 appearances for the Terriers he joined Preston North End, the club that wouldn't pay more than £250 for him when he was with St Helen's Town! Playing in the Second Division for the first time in his career, he helped North End win promotion before moving to Carlisle United where he became the club's player-manager. He later managed Stockport County and led the Edgeley Park club to the Third Division title in 1936-37.

KINDON, STEVE

After starring in Burnley's FA Youth Cup run of 1967-68, Steve Kindon became one of the first members of that victorious side to establish himself in the Clarets' first team. He made his debut in a 5-0

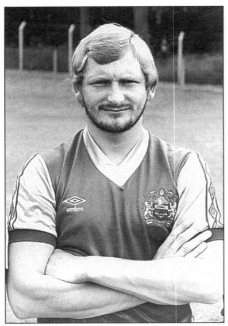

Steve Kindon, a member of Burnley's FA Youth cup winning side of 1967-68.

defeat at West Ham United in August 1968 but helped Burnley gain revenge two months later when he scored on his home debut in a 3-1 win over the Hammers. He was ever-present in the 1969-70 season and top-scored with 17 goals including a hat-trick in a 5-0 home win over Nottingham Forest. After the club were relegated in 1970-71, Kindon seemed to lose form and in the summer of 1972 he was transferred to Wolverhampton Wanderers for £100,000.

Despite scoring on his debut, Kindon took time to settle and only appeared briefly during the Molineux club's run to the League Cup Final in 1974. Though the club were relegated in 1975-76, they won the Second Division Championship the following season with Kindon playing his part. He had scored 31 goals in 167 first team outings for Wolves when in November 1977 he returned to Turf Moor for £80,000.

He spent two more seasons with the Clarets, taking his tally of goals to 58 in 225 games before joining Huddersfield Town. After helping the Terriers win the Fourth Division Championship, top-scoring with 18 goals, a serious knee injury brought his playing career to a premature end.

L

LARGEST CROWD

Turf Moor housed its largest crowd for the FA Cup third round match against Huddersfield Town on 23 February 1924. A crowd of 54,775 saw the Clarets win 1-0, courtesy of a Walter Weaver goal.

LATE FINISHES

Burnley's final match of the season against Millwall at Turf Moor on 7 June 1947 is the latest date for the finish of any Clarets' season. The game ended all-square at 1-1 with Billy Morris netting for Burnley.

LATEST GOAL

Geoff Nulty is credited with the latest Football League goal ever. He equalised for Burnley in the match against Ipswich Town on 27 March 1971. The game, which ended all-square at 2-2, saw Nulty's goal officially timed at one second from the end!

LEAGUE GOALS – CAREER HIGHEST

George Beel holds the Turf Moor record for the most League goals with a career total of 178 goals between 1923 and 1932.

LEAGUE GOALS – LEAST CONCEDED

During the 1897-98 season, the Clarets conceded just 24 goals in winning the Second Division Championship. That was from a 30-match programme but the club's best from a 42-match campaign is 29 in 1946-47 when the Clarets were runners-up in the Second Division.

LEAGUE GOALS – MOST INDIVIDUAL

George Beel holds the Burnley record for the most league goals in a season with 35 in 1927-28 when the Clarets finished 19th in the First Division.

LEAGUE GOALS – MOST SCORED

Burnley's highest goals tally in the Football League was during the 1960-61 season when they scored 102 goals in finishing fourth in Division One.

LEAGUE VICTORY – HIGHEST

The club's best victory in the Football League came on 9 January 1892 when the Clarets beat Darwen 9-0 with Tommy Nicol and Alex

McLardie both scoring hat-tricks and Jack Hill two goals, whilst John Espie also got his name on the scoresheet.

LEYLAND DAF CUP

The Leyland Daf Cup replaced the Sherpa Van Trophy for the 1989-90 season. The club lost both of their group games, 3-0 at Preston North End and 2-0 at home to Stockport County. In 1990-91 the Clarets beat Crewe Alexandra 2-1 and drew 1-1 at Stockport County to qualify for the knockout stages of the competition. In the first round, the Clarets were drawn at home to the Edgeley Park club and won 3-2 with goals from Eli, Jakub and White. A Ron Futcher goal was enough to beat Bradford City in round two but the Clarets then suffered a humiliating 6-1 defeat at Preston North End in the third round.

LINDLEY, DICK

Dick Lindley played his early football playing for Oswaldtwistle Rovers before being signed by Burnley in March 1908. He made his league debut in the third match of the 1908-09 season, scoring Burnley's second goal in a 2-0 win over Derby County. However, it was 1911-12 before he established himself as a first team regular

in the Burnley side, scoring 15 goals in 34 games including a hat-trick in a 5-1 home win over Hull City. Forming a prolific partnership with Bert Freeman, he netted another hat-trick in a 5-0 win over Clapton Orient as the Clarets won promotion to the First Division in 1912-13. The following season he won an FA Cup winners' medal as Burnley beat Liverpool 1-0 at the Crystal Palace. He was still a member of the Burnley side when League football resumed after the First World War but after taking his tally of goals to 46 in 152 games, he left to play for Bradford City. After just one season at Valley Parade, he joined Coventry City where he ended his league career.

LOCHHEAD, ANDY

A striker with a deadly finish, Andy Lochhead began his league career with Burnley, having joined the Turf Moor club from the Renfrew club in Paisley. He made his debut in a 3-1 home defeat by Manchester City in August 1960 before scoring twice in his second game as the Clarets drew 4-4 with Chelsea. Despite this early promise, it was 1962-63 before he established himself fully in the Burnley side, top scoring with 19 goals in 32 games. He led the way again the following season, netting four goals for the club in a 6-1 win over Manchester United. In 1963-64 he formed a formidable partnership with Willie Irvine, the two of them scoring 43 of the club's 69 goals. Lochhead's total of 21 included five goals in the final game of the season when Chelsea were beaten 6-2 and a hat-trick in a 4-2 win at Blackpool. Lochhead netted another five goals in a match for the Clarets the following season as Bournemouth were defeated 7-0 in an FA Cup third round replay. He also netted a hat-trick in a 4-0 League Cup win at Doncaster Rovers. In 1966-67 he again topped the Burnley scoring charts with 18 goals, his total including all four in a 4-2 home win over Aston Villa. He went on to score 128 goals in 266 games before joining Leicester City.

He appeared in the 1969 FA Cup Final for the Filbert Street club before moving to Aston Villa in February 1970. He played in the League Cup Final the following year and in 1971-72 won a Third Division Championship medal. That season he headed the club's goalscoring charts with 19 including a hat-trick in a 6-0 win at Oldham Athletic, the club he joined after leaving Villa Park in the summer of 1973. After Oldham, he played in the NASL before returning to Boundary Park as coach and then Turf Moor as scout.

LORD, BOB

Local butcher Bob Lord became one of football's most controversial characters. He was chairman of Burnley Football Club for 26 years and a leading light of the Football League. He ignored his fellow directors and bought 80 acres of farmland where the Gawthorpe training ground was built. Here the club set up a youth scheme, which soon became the envy of the top flight clubs.

Lord also set about modernising Turf Moor and in 1967 work began on an £180,000 stand which seated 4,500 at the Cricket Field End. This was officially opened by Bob Lord's friend, Prime Minister Edward Heath on 23 November 1973, four years after it had first housed spectators. The Bob Lord Stand replaced the pre-1914 Main Stand and this too was opened by Edward Heath in September 1974.

Bob Lord wasn't popular with everyone connected with Burnley

Football Club but when he died from cancer on 8 December 1981, his death left a big gap in the game.

LOWEST

The lowest number of goals scored by Burnley in a single Football League season is 29 in 1970-71 when the club finished 21st in the First Division and were relegated. The club's lowest points record in the Football League occurred in 1889-90 when the Clarets gained just 13 points from their 22-match programme.

McCLUGGAGE, ANDY

Full-back Andy McCluggage played his early football for Cliftonville in his native Ireland before being transferred to Bradford Park Avenue in 1921. His performances for the Yorkshire club led to him winning the first of 12 caps when he played against England in 1923. He joined Burnley in the summer of 1925 and made his debut in the 10-0 defeat at Aston Villa on the opening day of the 1925-26 season. Despite this disastrous start to his Turf Moor career, McCluggage went on to be a regular first team member for six seasons, missing very few games.

He made a further 11 appearances for Ireland, scoring his only international goal in a 2-2 draw with Wales in 1929. He had scored 24 goals in 213 games for Burnley when after a short spell with Dundalk, he joined Preston North End.

His first game for the Lilywhites was against Burnley at Turf Moor on Christmas Day 1931 when the teams shared four goals. He played in just three games for the Deepdale club before leaving to play non-League football for Morecambe.

McDONALD, COLIN

One of Burnley's greatest goalkeepers, Colin McDonald had to wait almost six years after joining the club before making his first team debut. In April 1954 he replaced Des Thompson in a Clarets' side beaten 5-1 by Aston Villa. Despite that result, he kept his place for the remaining four games of the campaign and was the club's first-choice 'keeper for the next five seasons. He was ever-present in 1955-56 when the club finished seventh in Division One and the following season represented the Football League in a 4-1 win over the Scottish League. He made his full international debut in May 1958 as England played the Soviet Union prior to the World Cup in Sweden. He played in all England's World Cup games, producing an outstanding display in a goalless draw against the eventual world champions, Brazil.

Sadly, McDonald's career came to a premature end when he broke a leg whilst playing for the Football League against the Irish League in Dublin on 17 March 1959, though no-one knew it at the time. He spent the League Championship-winning season of 1959-60 playing in the Central League team but in the summer of 1961 after playing in 201 League and Cup games, he was forced to quit league football.

After coaching at Wycombe Wanderers, he worked as a chief scout for Bury before attempting to resurrect his playing career with non-League Altrincham. Things didn't work out and after a spell as Bolton's chief scout, he rejoined Bury as Administration Manager before becoming the club's General Manager. He later coached both Oldham Athletic and Tranmere Rovers.

McILROY, JIMMY

Burnley have always been noted for their ability to find stars without breaking the bank, but they can not have made a better investment than the £7,000 they paid Glentoran for Jimmy McIlroy. Born at Lambeg near Belfast, he made his senior debut with Glentoran in the last game of the 1948-49 season as well as winning Irish Youth international honours.

At Burnley he became recognised as one of the most accomplished inside-forwards of the post-war era. Northern Ireland capped him for the first time in October 1951 and he subsequently enjoyed one run of 34 consecutive appearances.

McIlroy was a natural player, rarely caught in possession – a cool performer with plenty of time on the ball. His great strength was the consistency of service to the centre-forward and largely because of that, he became the architect of the great Burnley side of the late 1950s and early 1960s. Even so, he could also find the net and scored

Jimmy McIlroy, Burnley's greatest-ever player.

hat-tricks against New Brighton (Home 9-0) in the FA Cup competition of 1956-57 and Leicester City (Home 7-3) in 1957-58.

McIlroy was an intelligent playmaker, a classical scheming inside-forward. He enjoyed splendid partnerships with Jimmy Adamson for Burnley and Danny Blanchflower for Northern Ireland. With Docherty as manager, McIlroy and Blanchflower masterminded Northern Ireland to their greatest heights in the 1958 World Cup. They reached the quarter-finals with McIlroy forming a devastating partnership with Peter McParland the Aston Villa winger.

McIlroy's influence played a major role in Burnley's Championship triumph of 1959-60. After winning a League Championship medal and an FA Cup finalists' medal with Burnley, mist people thought he was going to end his playing career with the Turf Moor outfit. But after scoring 131 goals in 497 games he was placed on the transfer list and in March 1963 joined Stoke City for £25,000.

He made an immediate impact on his arrival at the Victoria Ground, helping the Potters to clinch the Second Division title in 1962-63. His new found form with Stoke led to him being recalled into the Northern Ireland team in 1966 after a three-year absence. He represented his country on 55 occasions, scoring 10 goals, including one in Northern Ireland's historic victory at Wembley in 1957.

After finishing his career back in Lancashire with Oldham, he returned to Stoke as chief coach. He resigned his position there in 1969 and was out of the game until 4 November 1970 when he was appointed team manager at Bolton. Incredibly after only 18 days in charge, he parted company with the club. He returned to Burnley where he became a much respected sports journalist.

McLINTOCK, TOM

After playing his early football with a number of junior clubs in the Glasgow area, left-back Tom McLintock joined Clyde before being transferred to Kilmarnock. He joined Burnley in the summer of 1892 but had to wait until the opening game of the 1893-94 season before making his debut as Burnley lost 3-2 at Newton Heath. After that, McLintock was a virtual ever-present for seven seasons and in 1897-98 won a Second Division Championship medal with the Clarets.

Strong in the tackle and a good distributor of the ball, he was unlucky not to win full international honours for Scotland. During the 1900-01 season, McLintock lost his place in the Burnley defence to George Lockhart who had joined the club from Bolton Wanderers. He continued to play for the club for the next two seasons, proving himself to be a versatile performer, appearing at left-half, centre-forward and outside-left. On 13 April 1901, he was wearing the Number 11 shirt when he scored all four goals including two penalties in a 4-0 defeat of Blackpool.

He had scored 14 goals in 254 games for the Turf Moor club before being transferred back to Kilmarnock in 1903.

MANAGERS

Below is a complete list of Burnley's full-time managers with the inclusive dates during which they held office:

Arthur Sutcliffe	1893-1896	Joe Brown	1976-1977
Harry Bradshaw	1896-1899	Harry Potts	1977-1979
Ernest Mangnall	1900-1903	Brian Miller	1979-1983
Spen Whittaker	1903-1910	Frank Casper	1983
John Haworth	1910-1924	John Bond	1983-1984
Albert Pickles	1925-1932	John Benson	1984-1985
Tom Bromilow	1932-1935	Martin Buchan	1985
Alf Boland	1935-1940	Tommy Cavanagh	1985-1986
Cliff Britton	1945-1948	Brian Miller	1986-1989
Frank Hill	1948-1954	Frank Casper	1989-1991
Alan Brown	1954-1957	Jimmy Mullen	1991-1996
Billy Dougall	1957-1958	Adrian Heath	1996-1997
Harry Potts	1958-1970	Chris Waddle	1997-1998
Jimmy Adamson	1970-1976	Stan Ternant	1998-

MANGNALL, ERNEST

Bolton-born Ernest Mangnall kept goal for the Lancashire County side, won road races as cyclist and was a good cross-country runner who represented Bolton Harriers. A director of Bolton Wanderers, he arrived at Turf Moor in 1899 to take over as the club's secretary-manager following the departure of Harry Bradshaw. However, at the end of his first season the club were relegated and though they finished third in Division Two in 1901-02, they were bottom of the table the following season when the Clarets had to apply for re-election.

Mangnall left Turf Moor at the end of that season to take charge at Manchester United. He gained promotion in 1906 and brought two League Championships to the club in 1908 and 1911 as well as the FA Cup in 1909.

He left Old Trafford in 1912 to manage Manchester City. His best season at Maine Road was 1920-21 when the club were runners-up in the First Division. A founder of the Central League and the man largely responsible for the formation of the Football Managers' Association, he was awarded a long-service medal by the FA in 1921 after 21 years service to football.

MARATHON MATCH

During the FA Cup competition of 1955-56, Burnley were involved in five matches against Chelsea in the fourth round. The first match at Turf Moor ended all-square at 1-1 with Peter McKay netting for the Clarets. In the replay at Stamford Bridge, a Brian Pilkington goal gave Burnley a 1-1 draw after extra-Time. The third meeting between the clubs was played at St Andrew's but that too ended all-square at 2-2 after extra-time with McIlroy and McKay the Clarets' scorers. The clubs met again at Highbury a week later but the game was goalless and so they met for a fifth time at White Hart Lane 48 hours later. This time Chelsea ran out winners 2-0 after a tie lasting 510 minutes!

MARKSMEN – LEAGUE

Burnley's top league goalscorer is George Beel who struck 178 goals during his nine years at Turf Moor. Only six players have hit more than 100 league goals for the club.

1.	George Beel	178
2.	Ray Pointer	118
3.	Jimmy McIlroy	116
4.	Louis Page	111
5.	Bert Freeman	103
6.	Andy Lochhead	101
7.	Bob Kelly	88
8.	John Connelly	86
9.	Jimmy Robson	79
10.	Willie Irvine	78

MARKSMEN – OVERALL

Eight players have hit a century of goals for Burnley. The club's top marksman is George Beel. The Century Club consists of:

1.	George Beel	187
2.	Ray Pointer	133
3.	Jimmy McIlroy	131
4.	Andy Lochhead	128
5=	Bert Freeman	115
	Louis Page	115
7.	John Connelly	105
8.	Jimmy Robson	100

MATCH OF THE DAY

Burnley's first appearance on BBC's 'Match of the Day' was on 24 September 1966 when they lost 4-1 at Manchester United with Andy Lochhead scoring the Clarets' goal.

MATHER, HAROLD

Bolton-born full-back Harold Mather was wanted by his home-town club but decided to join Burnley when the Turf Moor club offered him terms in May 1938. As with many players, the Second World War interrupted his progress and though he appeared in 132 wartime games for the Clarets, he had to wait until the opening game of the 1946-47 season before making his Football League debut in a 1-1 home draw against Coventry City. That season Mather was ever-present as Burnley won promotion to the First Division and reached the FA Cup Final where they lost 1-0 to Charlton Athletic.

Over the next seven seasons, Mather missed very few games, taking his total of first team appearances to 329. His last game was against Leicester City (Home 3-1) on 6 September 1954.

On leaving Turf Moor he became player-coach at Nelson before joining Hull City as the Yorkshire club's coach. He then had a spell as player-manager of Kettering Town before holding a number of coaching posts in South Africa. When he returned to these shores he became player-manager of Nelson before hanging up his boots.

MILLER, BRIAN

Brian Miller, who played out of positon during his only appearance for England.

Brian Miller made his Burnley debut during the club's marathon FA Cup tie against Chelsea at Stamford Bridge on 1 February 1956. It was the following campaign before he became a regular in the Burnley side, keeping his place for the next 11 seasons. When the club won the League Championship in 1959-60, Miller was ever-present, his form that season earning him selection for the England Under-23 side. After another successful season in 1960-61 Miller won his only full cap when he played for England against Austria in Vienna in May 1961. Unfortunately, Miller was asked to play at right-half in a match England lost 3-1.

Miller went on to play in 455 games for the Clarets, scoring 37 goals, two of which came in the two-legged European Fairs Cup match against Eintrackt Frankfurt in 1966-67. Only four days after the second-leg of that tie, Miller twisted a knee in a 1-0 win at Aston Villa – an injury that ended his playing career.

At the end of that season, he joined the Turf Moor club's coaching staff before replacing Harry Potts as manager in October 1979. Miller was in charge in 1981-82 when the Clarets won the Third Division Championship but was dismissed in January 1983 with the club struggling in the lower reaches of the Second Division.

In the summer of 1986, Miller was asked to manage the club for a second time. The following season the Clarets were knocked out of the FA Cup by Telford and just managed to stave off relegation to the Vauxhall Conference. In 1987-88 he led the club to the Sherpa Van Trophy Final at Wembley but lost his position to Frank Casper in January 1989. He then took up a new position within the club as the Clarets' chief scout.

MOFFAT, HUGH

Hugh Moffat played his early football for his home-town sides, Congleton Town and Congleton Swifts before signing for Burnley in January 1904. Equally at home at left-back or left-half, he made his debut for the Clarets in a 2-2 home draw against Barnsley three months after his arrival at Turf Moor. After that, he was a virtual ever-present in the Burnley side for the next six seasons, playing in 214 League and Cup games for the club.

After losing his first team place to Billy Watson, who joined the club from Southport Central in 1909, Moffat left Turf Moor to join Oldham Athletic. During his first season at Boundary Park, he helped the club win promotion to the First Division and in 1914-15 when it looked likely that the Latics would win the League Championship, a 2-1 defeat against Burnley left the former Clarets' player and his team-mates one point behind champions, Everton.

When league football resumed after the First World War, Moffat had a season playing for Chesterfield before returning to Congleton Town where he ended his playing days.

MORGAN, WILLIE

A Scottish Schoolboy triallist when playing for Fishcross Boys' Club at Sauchie near Alloa in 1959, he signed as an amateur for Burnley in May 1960. He turned professional the following year but had to wait until 1963 before he made his first team debut in a 1-0 win at Sheffield Wednesday. Morgan was a virtual ever-present in the Burnley side for the next five seasons, winning the first of 21 caps for Scotland against Northern Ireland in October 1967.

By now, his wing play was attracting the attention of a number of clubs and he decided that he needed to leave Turf Moor to benefit his career. The club refused his transfer request and so his own game began to deteriorate. His lowest ebb must have been when the Burnley

club refused to let him play in any of the sides and banned him from the training ground.

However, in August 1968, Manchester United paid £117,000 to take him to Old Trafford. Although not renowned for his goalscoring ability, Morgan nevertheless created many for Best, Law, Charlton, Macari and Pearson. He did score a hat-trick in his first season with the club as Queen's Park Rangers were beaten 8-1. It was

Willie Morgan, seen here during his days with Bolton Wanderers.

United boss Frank O'Farrell who converted Morgan into a midfield role, from where he helped the Reds to take the Second Division title in 1974-75.

He returned to Burnley in the 1975 close season but after taking his total of appearances to 232 in which he scored 22 goals, he left to join Bolton Wanderers. After making his debut against Plymouth Argyle in March 1986, Morgan missed only three games up until May 1979. During his time at Bolton they became one of the classiest sides in the Second Division and won the title in 1977-78.

In November 1978, Morgan was at the centre of a court sensation when Tommy Docherty, his former manager at United brought a libel action against him and Granada TV. The action collapsed when Docherty admitted that he had lied in court.

Whilst at Bolton he twice played in the NASL for Minnesota Kicks. His last game in Bolton colours came against United at Old Trafford, after which he left to join Blackpool where he ended his playing career.

MORRIS, BILLY

Billy Morris joined Burnley from Llandudno Town in January 1939 and went straight into the Clarets' first team for the match against Norwich City, which Burnley won 3-0. He had just established himself in the Burnley side when war was declared. During the hostilities, Morris was a sergeant in the Army and served in the Far East.

In 1946-47 he helped Burnley win promotion to the First Division and appeared in the FA Cup Final against Charlton Athletic. During the course of that season he netted the first of three hat-tricks for the club in a 3-0 win at Coventry City. He gained the first of five full caps for Wales against Scotland in 1947. His best season for Burnley was 1951-52 when he top scored with 18 goals including a hat-trick in a 7-1 win over Middlesborough and four goals in a 6-1 defeat of West Bromwich Albion. He went on to score 53 goals in 230 games before retiring from league football in 1952. After playing non-League football in Wales, he returned to Turf Moor as coach but in the summer of 1960 he was appointed manager of Wrexham. After losing his job after just one season he returned to take charge for another brief spell in the mid-sixties before being relieved of his duties for a second time.

MORRISON, TOM

Tom Morrison joined Burnley from Glentoran in February 1894 and made his debut in a 1-0 defeat at Wolves the following month. The Irish-born winger scored on his home debut the following week in a 3-1 win over Derby County but after just seven league appearances, left Turf Moor and returned home. He rejoined Glentoran and in March 1895, he won the first of three full caps for his country . He returned to Turf Moor towards the end of the 1896-97 season but couldn't prevent the Clarets being relegated for the first time in their history.

The following season he helped Burnley win the Second Division Championship and promotion to the top flight via the Test Matches. His partnership with newly-signed Jimmy Ross was a revelation with the Irishman's crosses providing many of the Scotsman's 23 goals. In 1898-99 Burnley finished third in Division One after leading the table for part of the season with Morrison once again in outstanding form on the right-wing. He took his total of international caps for Ireland to seven and his tally of goals to 28 in 194 games for Burnley before leaving to play for Manchester United.

He returned to Turf Moor for a third time in 1904, this time as the club's trainer-coach. In September 1906 he did appear in the 2-0 defeat at Leicester Fosse following an injury crisis at the club before later returning to his first club Glentoran as their coach.

MOSSCROP, ERNIE

Southport-born Ernie Mosscrop joined Burnley from his home-town team, Southport Central in the summer of 1912. He made his first team debut for the Clarets in a 2-1 home win over Glossop on the opening day of the season. In that 1912-13 season, Mosscrop scored four goals in 22 games from his position on the right-wing as the club won promotion from the Second Division. Midway through the following season he switched to outside-left and played an important role in helping the Clarets reach the FA Cup Final where they beat Liverpool 1-0. His form led to him winning two full caps for England and in 1914-15, his pin-point crosses led to numerous chances for Freeman and Hodgson.

When league football resumed in 1919-20, Mosscrop was still the club's first-choice outside-left but the following season when Burnley won the League Championship he lost his place to Walt Weaver who had been signed from South Liverpool. He regained his place the following season and went on to score 20 goals in 198 League and Cup games before a serious illness forced his premature retirement.

MOST GOALS IN A SEASON

When Burnley came fourth in Division One in 1960-61, they scored 102 goals in 42 matches.

MOST MATCHES

Burnley played their most number of first-class matches, 62, in 1960-61. This comprised 42 league games, seven FA Cup games, eight League Cup games, four European Cup games and an appearance in the FA Charity Shield.

MULLEN, JIMMY

Jarrow-born Jimmy Mullen was a defender with Sheffield Wednesday and in 10 years with the Hillsborough club, appeared in 230 League games. He then joined Rotherham United and captained them to the Third Division Championship in 1980-81. Mullen's third club was Cardiff City and in 1982-83 he skippered the Bluebirds to promotion from the Third Division as runners-up to Portsmouth. After a spell as assistant-manager with the Ninian Park club, he joined Newport County as player-manager, later becoming assistant-manager at Aberdeen.

Following the departure of Sam Ellis at Blackpool, Mullen was asked to take charge of the team for the last five games of the 1988-89 season and after they won four of those matches and so avoid relegation, he was appointed on an permanent basis. In 1989-90 the club seemed to be fixed to the foot of the Third Division and within 11 months of taking charge, his contract was terminated.

Mullen was appointed Burnley manager in October 1991, having been at the club since August 1990 when he became Frank Casper's assistant. His start as Clarets' manager was sensational as the club recorded nine straight league wins and nine successive victories away from home. At the end of his first season in charge, Burnley won the Fourth Division League Championship. He led the club to the play-offs in 1993-94 where they beat Stockport County in the Wembley final to win promotion for the second time in three years. After the club were relegated after one season in the First Division, their dismal form continued and in February 1996 he parted company with the club.

N

NESBITT, BILLY

Billy Nesbitt joined the Clarets from Hebden Bridge FC in September 1911 and though he made his debut in a 3-0 home win over Barnsley four months later, it was 1913-14 before he established himself as a first team regular. That season he was a member of the Burnley side that won the FA Cup for the first time in their history, his displays on the wing earning him selection for England in a trial match against the North. After the First World War, Nesbitt continued to be the club's first-choice right-winger and in 1920-21 his partnership with Bob Kelly was instrumental in the club's success in winning the League Championship.

Nesbitt went on to score 20 goals in 192 League and Cup games though a series of niggling injuries ruined his last couple of seasons with the club. He joined Bristol City in the hope of resurrecting his career but sadly injuries forced his retirement from the game.

NEUTRAL GROUNDS

Turf Moor has been used as a neutral ground for FA Cup matches on a number of occasions and in 1922 hosted the semi-final match between Huddersfield Town and Notts Count. A crowd of 46,323 saw the Yorkshire club win 3-1. In 1927 Turf Moor housed its only international match when England played Wales. Burnley players Louis Page and Jack Hill were in the England side but Hill put through his own goal as Wales won 2-1.

Burnley themselves have had to replay on a neutral ground a number of times:

Date	Opponents	Venue	FA Cup	Score
02.04.1913	Sunderland	St Andrew's	Semi-Final	2-3
01.04.1914	Sheffield.U.	Goodison Park	Semi-Final	1-0
12.04.1947	Liverpool	Maine Road	Semi-Final	1-0
06.,02.1956	Chelsea	St Andrew's	Round 4	2-2
13.02.1956	Chelsea	Highbury	Round 4	0-0
15.02.1956	Chelsea	White Hart Lane	Round 4	0-2
09.04.1962	Fulham	Filbert Street	Semi-Final	2-1

The club's semi-finals in the FA Cup were of course played on a neutral ground and they were as follows:

Date	Opponents	Venue	Score
29.03.1913	Sunderland	Bramall Lane	0-0
28.03.1914	Sheffield United	Old Trafford	0-0
29.03.1924	Aston Villa	Bramall Lane	0-3
16.03.1935	Sheffield Wednesday	Villa Park	0-3
29.03.1947	Liverpool	Ewood Park	0-0
18.03.1961	Tottenham Hotspur	Villa Park	0-3
31.03.1962	Fulham	Villa Park	1-1
30.04.1974	Newcastle United	Hillsborough	0-2

The club were also forced to play on a neutral ground in two League Cup semi-final replays after the two legs had ended all-square on aggregate. In 1960-61, Burnley lost 2-1 to Aston Villa at Old Trafford and in 1968-69 went down 3-2 to Swindon Town at the Hawthorns. The club's appearances in the FA Cup Final at the Crystal Palace and Wembley as well as the Sherpa Van Trophy Final also qualify for inclusion.

NEWTON, KEITH

Keith Newton was a member of the successful Blackburn Rovers FA Youth Cup-winning side of 1959. Newton made his first team debut for Rovers in the left-half position but soon switched to left-back, making the position his own. Sharp in the tackle and sound in the air, he was noted for his attacking runs down the flank. He finally settled into the right-back position and won his first major honour in 1964 when he gained the first of several England Under-23 caps against Scotland at Newcastle. Shortly after this he suffered the first of sev-

Keith Newton, a virtual ever-present in his six seasons at Turf Moor.

eral major injuries that dogged his career and cost him many representative honours. He injured a knee in training with England and had to have a cartilage operation. Once fully recovered he won his first full cap_ against West Germany but just before the interval he was carried from the field with a suspected broken leg. Thankfully the injury turned out to be less serious than feared but they did hamper his early career and he just missed out on inclusion for the 1966 World Cup. By 1969 Newton was a world-rated player, though Rovers were struggling in the lower reaches of Division Two.

In December 1969 after appearing in 306 league games for the Ewood Park club, he joined Everton for £80,000 and helped them win the 1969-70 League Championship. He became unsettled at the way he was being asked to play and after losing his place, joined Burnley on a free transfer in the summer of 1972.

After making his debut in a 2-2 draw at Carlisle United on the opening day of the 1972-73 season, he went on to become one of six ever-presents as the Clarets won the Second Division Championship. A cool, cultured and vastly experienced full-back, he missed very few games in six seasons at Turf Moor and had appeared in 252 League and Cup games before finally bowing out at the end of the 1977-78 season.

He later had brief spells in non-League football with Morecambe and Clitheroe. Sadly, he passed away in the summer of 1998.

NICKNAMES

Burnley's nickname is 'The Clarets'. Many players in the club's history have been fondly known by their nickname including:

Tom Morrison	1894-1906	Ching
Ronnie Hornby	1934-1948	Dipper
Bob Brocklebank	1935-1939	The Toff
Jackie Chew	1946-1954	Cowboy
Gordon Harris	1958-1968	Bomber
Steve Kindon	1968-1972/1977-1980	Skippy

NICOL, TOM

Born in Broxburn, right-winger Tom Nicol signed for Burnley in 1890 after playing local football in his native Scotland. His first game for the Turf Moor club was against Preston North End towards the end of the 1890-91 season when he scored a at-trick in a 6-2 home win. The following season, his first full campaign for the Clarets, he was the club's leading scorer with 17 goals in 25 games including a hat-trick in the 9-0 home win over Darwen. Over the next six season, Nicol showed his versatility by playing in a variety of positions but was wearing the Number 7 shirt when he netted his third hat-trick for the club in a 6-0 home win over Blackburn Rovers in April 1896.

He had scored 44 goals in 149 games for Burnley when he left Turf Moor to join Blackburn Rovers in December 1896 for a fee of £105. After just one season at Ewood Park he was transferred to Southampton where he was converted into a dashing, fearless right-back. When his playing days were over, he became landlord of the Kingsland Tavern in the town.

NOBLE, PETER

Joe Harvey took Peter Noble to Newcastle United from Consett in November 1964 and gave him his first league chance at Chelsea ten months later. During the 1966-67 season he scored seven goals in just 15 First Division games but had appeared only once the following season when in January 1968,he was sold to Swindon Town for £8,000. He contributed 20 League and Cup goals to the Robins' successes of 1968-69 including the winning strike at Turf Moor in the

Peter Noble, one of the most popular players to represent the Turf Moor club.

League Cup semi-final re-play. He had scored 62 goals in 216 games for the Wiltshire club when Burnley paid £40,000 for his services at the end of May 1973.

An opening day injury to Mick Docherty gave him the chance to play at full-back during the 1973-74 campaign and he performed admirably as the Clarets finished sixth in Division One. The following season he scored the first of four hat-tricks for the club in a 4-1 home win over his former club, Newcastle United. Noble was the club's top scorer in 1975-76, scoring all four goals in a 4-4 home draw with Norwich City and a hat-trick in a 4-1 defeat of Middlesborough. He topped the club's scoring charts in 1976-77 and 1978-79, netting his fourth hat-trick in the latter season as the Clarets beat Fulham 5-3. Nobel had scored 80 goals in 300 games, of which 18 were penalties before being somewhat prematurely sold to Blackpool for £25,000.

Despite scoring on his debut for the Seasiders, he never really settled at Bloomfield Road and decided to hang up his boots after being released by the club in May 1983.

NON-LEAGUE

Burnley have played non-League opposition in the FA Cup on a number of occasions. The most recent was the first round match at Stafford Rangers on 17 November 1990, which the Clarets won 3-1.

The club's record against non-League clubs in the FA Cup since they joined the Football League is as follows:

Date	Opposition	Venue	Stage	Score
02.02.1889	Old Westminsters	Home	Round 1	4-3
14.12.1901	Bishop Auckland	Away	Qualifying Rd	3-2
31.10.1903	Keswick	Away*	Qualifying Rd3	8-0
10.01.1920	Thorneycrofts	Away**	Round 1	0-0
13.01.1920	Thorneycrofts	Home	Round 1 (R)	5-0
26.01.1957	New Brighton	Home	Round 4	9-0
03.01.1975	Wimbledon	Home	Round 3	0-1
22.11.1980	Scarborough	Home	Round 1	1-0
21.11.1981	Runcorn	Home	Round 1	0-0
24.11.1981	Runcorn	Away	Round 1 (R)	2-1
18.01.1982	Altrincham	Home	Round 3	6-1
19.11.1983	Hyde United	Away*	Round 1	2-0
17.11.1984	Penrith	Away	Round 1	9-0
16.11.1985	Nuneaton Borough	Away	Round 1	3-2
15.11.1986	Telford	Away	Round 1	0-3
17.11.1990	Stafford Rangers	Away	Round 1	3-1

* Games switched to Turf Moor

**Game played at Fratton Park, Portsmouth

NULTY, GEOFF

Geoff Nulty was an apprentice on the books of Stoke City but after turning professional, failed to win a place in the Potters' first team and joined Burnley in the summer of 1968. He made his debut as a substitute for Dave Thomas in a 3-0 home win over Sunderland in August 1969. It was the Turf Moor club's relegation season of 1970-71 when Nulty finally established himself as a regular in the Clarets' side, showing his versatility by appearing in several different positions. After seemingly losing out to England international Keith Newton the following season, Nulty returned to the side in October 1972, replacing Dave Thomas

who had joined Queen's Park rangers. Nulty scored six goals in 35 games for the Clarets during the 1972-73 season as they won the Second Division Championship. Nulty impressed during the club's first season back in the top flight, being the Clarets' only ever-present. He had scored 24 goals in 152 games when he was transferred to Newcastle United for £130,000.

Manager Gordon Lee appointed him captain and though his goals helped the Magpies reach the League Cup Final in 1976, a broken jaw forced him to miss the Wembley match. After Newcastle were relegated, Nulty joined Everton for £40,000 but his career was eventually cut short when he was injured in a Merseyside derby and had to retire.

OLDEST PLAYER

The oldest player to line up in a Burnley first team is goalkeeper Jerry Dawson. He played the last of his 569 League and Cup games against Liverpool (Home 3-2) on Christmas Day 1928 at the age of 40 years 282 days.

O'NEIL, BRIAN

Known as the 'Bedlington Terrier' Brian O'Neil began his career with Burnley and was a member of the club's Central League Championship winning sides of 1961-62 and 1962-63. In April 1963 he made his first team debut in a 2-1 home win over West Bromwich Albion replacing Jimmy Adamson. For the next seven seasons, O'Neil was a virtual ever-present, always giving of his best when he wore the claret and blue. His performances for the Turf Moor club led to him winning international recognition with selection for the Football League and the England Under-23 side.

At the end of the 1969-70 season after which he had scored 25 goals in 282 League and Cup games, he was sold to Southampton for £75,000, then a club record for the Saints. Whilst Burnley were being relegated in 1970-71, O'Neil was ever-present in a Southampton side that finished seventh in Division One. He was an inspiration at The Dell and only a bad disciplinary record – he was suspended for nine weeks on one occasion – prevented him from winning full international honours.

He scored 18 goals in 166 games for the Saints but after they were relegated in 1974 he left to play for Third Division Huddersfield Town. He failed to prevent the Terriers from being relegated and after a season in the league's basement, he left Leeds Road to become player-manager of Bideford Town.

ORIENT

When Burnley entertained Orient on the final day of the 1986-87 season, they had to win to have a chance of remaining in the Fourth Division. Lincoln City had to lose to Swansea if they were to take the Clarets' place in the Vauxhall Conference.

A crowd of 15,696 were crammed inside Turf Moor for this most important of games. After both clubs had had chances to open the scoring, it was Neil Grewcock who put the Clarets ahead midway through the first-half. With news coming through that Lincoln were a goal down, it all seemed to be going Burnley's way especially when three minutes into the second-half, Ian Britton headed home the

Manager Brian Miller runs onto the pitch after Burnley's 2-1 victory

Clarets' second. Orient were pushing for a play-off place and on 56 minutes reduced the arrears when Comfort shot high into the roof of the Burnley net. Chances went begging at both ends but there was no further scoring and when the final whistle went, the pitch was invaded by hundreds of Burnley supporters celebrating the Clarets' survival.

OVERSON, VINCE

Powerfully built defender Vince Overson was on the verge of joining the Army when Burnley took him under their wing. He made his debut in a 2-1 home defeat by Orient in November 1979 and when he played his second game at Leicester City the following week, he created a piece of Burnley history. Playing alongside his brother Richard, it was the first time for 75 years that two brothers had played in the same Clarets' side.

In 1981-82 he won a Third Division Championship medal though an injury sustained towards the end of that successful campaign caused him to miss much of the 1982-83 season. Following Burnley's relegation to the Fourth Division in 1985, Overson made it clear that he didn't want to stay at Turf Moor and in June 1986 after scoring seven goals in 261 games he joined Birmingham City for £25,000.

His wholehearted approach to the game made him a great favourite with the fans but his relations with the St Andrew's club were not always amicable and after his wife went back to live in Burnley, being unable to settle in the Midlands, he went on the transfer list in the hope of moving back north.

After helping the club win the Leyland Daf Cup, he walked out and joined his former manager Lou Macari at Stoke City. He captained the Potters to the 'new' Second Division Championship in 1992-93 and though injuries caused him to miss a number of matches he had played in 216 first team games before returning to Turf Moor on a free transfer in August 1996.

OWN GOALS

There have been a number of instances of own goals over the years but there are two Burnley players whose misdemeanours stand out. Irish international left-back Alex Elder somehow managed to lob the ball over the advancing Adam Blacklaw from the most acute of angles to give Leeds United a 1-0 victory. That goal enabled the Yorkshire side to end the 1965-66 season as runners-up to Liverpool at the expense of the Clarets.

In the League Cup semi-final replay of 1968-69, Arthur Bellamy put through his own goal to enable Swindon Town to draw level. A few minutes later, future Claret, Peter Noble scored the winner for the Wiltshire club.

On the morning of their fifth round League Cup tie at Tottenham Hotspur on 19 January 1983, Burnley parted company with their manager Brian Miller. After a goalless first-half they conceded a goal after just 45 seconds of the second-half but then scored four times including two own goals by Graham Roberts to win 4-1.

P

PAGE, LOUIS

The only Burnley player ever to score a double hat-trick, Louis Page began his footballing career with South Liverpool before turning professional with Stoke in the summer of 1919. He joined Northampton Town in 1922 and in three seasons with the Cobblers, scored 26 goals in 129 League and Cup games.

He joined the Clarets in May 1925 with Jack Tresadern going to the County Ground as the club's player-manager. Page made his Burnley debut in the 10-0 defeat at Aston Villa on the opening day of the 1925-26 season and though the club were almost relegated, he was the Clarets' top scorer with 26 goals in 41 games. Included in that total were a hat-trick in a 6-3 home win over Leeds United and six goals in a 7-1 win at Birmingham, the first time he played at centre-forward. He continued to score for the club on a regular basis and formed a formidable partnership with George Beel. He netted another hat-trick for the club in April 1930 as the Clarets beat Liverpool 4-1. His performances for Burnley led to him winning seven full caps for England, though he only scored one goal for his country, that coming in the 9-1 demolition of Belgium in Brussels in May 1927.

Page, who was one of four brothers, all of whom played professional football, went on to score 115 goals in 259 League and Cup games before leaving to play for Manchester United in March 1932.

Unable to settle at Old Trafford, he joined Port Vale before becoming player-manager of Yeovil and Petters United. He later managed Newport County but his time there was unhappy and after a row over team selection he was suspended, then sacked. He later won damages for wrongful dismissal. During the Second World War, Page worked at Liverpool Docks and managed a local side called Carlton but in 1945 he became manager of Swindon Town. He almost led the Robins to promotion on two occasions and in 1947-48 helped plot the Clarets' downfall in that seasons FA Cup competition. He later managed Chester before scouting for Leicester City.

PEARCE, CHRIS

A Welsh Schoolboy international, goalkeeper Chris Pearce began his career as an apprentice with Wolverhampton Wanderers but on not being offered professional terms, he joined Blackburn Rovers. After loan spells with Rochdale, where he made his Football League debut and Barnsley, he joined the Spotland club on a permanent basis. In the summer of 1983 Pearce joined Port Vale on a free transfer but after playing in 48 League games for the Valiants he left to play for Wrexham. After just one season at the Racecourse Ground he left to sign for Burnley for £4,000.

He made his debut for the Clarets in a 3-0 defeat at Colchester United on the opening day of the 1987-88 season, a campaign in which he was ever-present. At the end of the season, he played for Burnley in the Sherpa Van Trophy Final and over the next four seasons missed very few games. After losing in the Division Four play-offs in 1990-91, the club won promotion the following season but Pearce found himself sharing the goalkeeping duties with four other players. At the end of that season, Pearce, who had played in 248 games, left Turf Moor to join Bradford City. After just nine appearances for the Bantams, back trouble forced his retirement from League football and he played non-League football for Chorley, Fleetwood and Accrington.

PENALTIES

The club's first-ever goal from the penalty spot was scored by Sandy Lang in a 3-2 win against West Bromwich Albion on 28 November 1891.

Burnley were awarded a record four penalties in their Division Two game against Grimsby Town on 13 February 1909. However, they also established two other records when they missed three of them and allowed the Grimsby goalkeeper Walter Scott to set a record of his own by saving three. The one penalty-kick that found its way into the net was scored by Billy Abbott and added to a previous goal, gave Burnley a 2-0 win.

Burnley's goalkeepers have also had their share of incidents relating to penalties. In February 1963, the Clarets were drawing 1-1 in a fourth round FA Cup replay against Liverpool at Anfield with just seconds of extra-Time remaining. The Clarets' Scottish international 'keeper Adam Blacklaw kicked a clearance straight to Ian St John and was then forced to upend the Liverpool forward as he prepared to shoot into an empty goal. From the resultant penalty, Ronnie Moran scored to send the Reds into the fifth round.

Harry Thomson saved a penalty on his debut in a 2-0 win at Leicester City in March 1965. Almost two years later, he saved another penalty and made countless outstanding saves as the Clarets drew 0-0 against Napoli in a third round second leg tie of the Inter Cities Fairs Cup.

PENDER, JOHN

Luton-born John Pender qualified for the Republic of Ireland through his parents and after joining Wolves as an apprentice and becoming a professional on his 18th birthday, won caps at both Youth and Under-21 level. He made his debut for Wolves against Swansea in March 1982 and became a regular in the Molineux club's side that won promotion to the First Division in 1982-83 but then suffered relegation in successive seasons. In the summer of 1985, Pender, who had appeared in 129 games for Wolves left to join Charlton Athletic for £35,000.

The Addicks had won promotion to the First Division at the end of Pender's first season with the club but in October 1987 he was on the move again, this time to Third Division Bristol City. Though he helped the Ashton Gate club to the semi-final of the League Cup, it wasn't long after that he lost his first team place and in September 1990 he joined Burnley for £70,000.

He made his debut for the Clarets in a 2-1 defeat at Stockport

County in September 1990 and in his first four seasons with the club, missed very few matches. In 1991-92 he captained the Turf Moor club to the Fourth Division title and two seasons later lifted the Endsleigh Trophy at Wembley after victory in the play-offs over Stockport County.

He had scored 10 goals in 230 games for Burnley when he left Turf Moor to join Wigan Athletic. He later moved to Rochdale where a severely damaged knee put his future playing career in jeopardy.

PHELAN, MIKE

Mike Phelan played his early football with Barrowford Celtic Boys' Club before joining Burnley as an apprentice in 1980. He made his first team debut at the age of 18 years 129 days in a 3-0 defeat at Chesterfield on 31 January 1981 when he came on as a substitute for Steve Taylor. The following month he won his first England Youth cap when he played against Northern Ireland in the European Championships.

In 1981-82 he played in 23 league games as the Clarets won the Third Division Championship but was ever-present when the club were instantly relegated the following season. Phelan missed very few games during his time at Turf Moor but in the summer of 1985 after scoring 13 goals in 220 games he was transferred to Norwich City for £60,000.

In his first season at Carrow Road, he helped the Canaries win the Second Division Championship. A first team regular for the next four seasons, he captained the club when they finished fourth in Division

Mike Phelan, seen here on England duty.

One in 1988-89. Phelan had played in 194 games for the Canaries when in the summer of 1989 he followed Steve Bruce to Manchester United. At the end of his first season at Old Trafford, he won an FA Cup winners' medal as United beat Crystal Palace after a replay. Also during that campaign he won his first England cap against Italy at Wembley. Another memorable season followed as United beat Barcelona in the final of the European Cup Winners' Cup. He won another FA Cup winners' medal in 1992 and in each of his last two seasons at Old Trafford, United won the Premier League as well as the FA Cup again in 1994.

Given a free transfer, he joined West Bromwich Albion before returning to Norwich City as reserve team coach.

PICKLES, ALBERT

Albert Pickles was elected to Burnley's board of directors in 1918. In his youth he had played football for Burnley Belvedere and was once offered a trial by Aston Villa but his parents would not give him permission to attend.

In January 1925 he replaced John Haworth as the club's secretary-manager but the Championship-winning side of 1920-21 was beginning to break-up and attendances too were falling. In his first full season in charge, the Clarets were beaten 10-0 by Aston Villa in their opening game and after having sold Bob Kelly, relegation was only avoided by Louis Page's double hat-trick at Birmingham. The club were eventually relegated in 1930 and there followed two seasons of undistinguished football before a 6-1 defeat at the hands of Preston North End, two games into the 1932-33 season, led to him tendering his resignation.

PILKINGTON, BRIAN

Brian Pilkington spent his entire Football League career playing in Lancashire. The Leyland-born winger began with his home-town team, Leyland Motors before Burnley signed him in April 1951. He made his debut in a 2-1 defeat at Tottenham Hotspur in September 1952 and the following season became the club's first-choice outside-left after Billy Elliott had been sold to Sunderland. His consistent form earned him his only full cap when he played for England against Northern Ireland in Belfast in October 1954. In March 1956 he scored his only hat-trick for the club in a 5-0 home win over Chelsea. He missed just one game during the club's League Championship winning season of 1959-60 but in March 1961 after having scored 77 goals in 340 games he was sold to Bolton Wanderers for £25,000.

Sadly, Pilkington did not reproduce the form that he had shown at Turf Moor and after being replaced by a young Dennis Butler, left Burnden Park to play for Bury. He later joined Barrow where he made 86 league appearances before moving to non-League Chorley in 1967. Injury forced his retirement in 1968 but the following year he rejoined his first club Leyland Motors and became their manager in 1970. He remained on the non-League scene and during the late 1970s returned to Chorley as manager.

PITCH

The Turf Moor pitch measures 114 yards by 72 yards.

Turf Moor – Burnley FC's ground

PLACE, WALTER Junior

Known as 'Little Walter' to distinguish himself from his older cousin, he played his early football for local sides Blue Stars and Union Stars before signing for Burnley in 1893. His first game for the club was in a 2-0 defeat at Bolton Wanderers in January 1894. Place became a first team regular in 1894-95 forming an exciting left-wing partnership with Billy Bowes and though the club were relegated after the Test Matches in 1896-97, Place helped them bounce straight back the following season. In that 1897-98 season, the Burnley-born winger scored seven goals and created many chances for Ross, Toman and Bowes. During the 1899-1900 season, Place, who had scored 34 goals in 167 games, lost his place in the side and followed manager Harry Bradshaw to Woolwich Arsenal.

He soon established himself in the side at Plumstead and in 1901-02 helped the Gunners to their then highest-ever League position of fourth in Division Two. He later left the club after his contract was cancelled.

PLACE, WALTER Senior

'Big Walter' as he was known first appeared in the Burnley side in 1886 when he was just 16 years old. However, he moved on to play for both Colne and Bacup before returning to Turf Moor for the start of the 1890-91 season. One of the club's earliest utility players, he made his league debut at outside-left in a 3-1 defeat at Wolverhampton Wanderers.

He wore almost every outfield shirt for the Clarets and even started two League games in goal because of injury to Jack Hillman but both resulted in defeats – Blackburn Rovers (Away 2-3) and Everton (Away 3-4). Though he played for the club for almost ten years, he never really established himself in any position, although he preferred right-half. When he left the club in 1900, he had scored nine goals in 149 games.

Walter Place senior was a great all-round sportsman, capable of holding his own at athletics, snooker, cricket bowls and shooting, whilst he was also recognised as England's best wrestler following an international tournament at Blackburn.

PLASTIC

Four Football League clubs have replaced their normal grass playing pitches with artificial surfaces at one stage or another. Queen's Park Rangers were the first in 1981 but the Loftus Road plastic was discarded in 1988 in favour of a return to turf. Luton Town, Oldham Athletic and Preston North End followed. The Clarets never played on the Boundary Park plastic but lost 3-2 on 2 October 1982 on their only visit to Loftus Road with Trevor Steven scoring both goals for Burnley. The club suffered successive defeats in 1985-86 and 1986-87 when visiting Deepdale but gained a 1-1 draw when visiting Luton Town's Kenilworth Road plastic in a second round League Cup match in 1988-89. Paul Comstive scored from the penalty spot for the Clarets, who lost 1-0 to the Hatters in the replay!

PLAY-OFFS

Burnley have been involved in the divisional play-offs on two occasions. In 1990-91 the club finished sixth in Division Four and met Torquay United over two-legs. After losing 2-0 at Plainmoor, the Clarets could only manage a 1-0 win at home, their goal being scored by Torquay's Evans and so failed to qualify for the play-off final.

In 1993-94, the Clarets finished sixth in the 'new' Division Two and so played third placed Plymouth Argyle. A crowd of 18,794 saw the two sides play out a goalless draw at Turf Moor after which it seemed as if the advantage lay with the Devon club. Two goals from John Francis and another from Warren Joyce gave Burnley a 3-1 win and a place in the Wembley final against Stockport County. Despite going a goal behind after two minutes when Chris Beaumont scored with a diving header, Burnley battled hard. Mike Wallace, County's defender was sent-off after 13 minutes and a quarter-of-an-hour later, David Eyres equalised for the Clarets. County's goalscorer Chris Beaumont was sent-off after 61 minutes to leave the Edgeley Park club with nine men. Four minutes later, Gary Parkinson scored Burnley's second and what turned out to be winning goal to take the Clarets into the First Division.

POINTER, RAY

Ray Pointer made his league debut for Burnley on 5 October 1957 in a

3-2 defeat at Luton Town five days before his 21st birthday. He scored on his home debut the following week as Sunderland were beaten 6-0 and ended the campaign with 10 goals in 25 games. In 1958-59 his first full season for the club he was the Clarets' top scorer with 27 goals in 37 league games. The following season when Burnley won the League Championship, Pointer played in every League and Cup game, scoring 23 goals including a hat-trick in a 5-2 win at Arsenal. On 16 September 1961, Pointer netted his second hat-trick for the club in a 6-2 win at Birmingham City, his prolific marksmanship earning him his first full England cap some 12 days later. Leading his country's attack, he found the net in a 4-1 win over Luxembourg at Highbury. In 1961-2, Pointer scored 26 goals as he had the previous season and played for the Clarets in the FA Cup Final defeat against Tottenham Hotspur.

In April 1963 he chipped a one in his foot in the match at Nottingham Forest and though he took his tally of goals to 133 in 270 games before leaving to join Bury in December 1965, he was never the same player. After scoring 17 goals in 19 games he was on the move again, this time to Coventry City but with the Sky Blues on their way to their first-ever promotion, he joined Portsmouth. At Fratton Park he combined his playing duties with coaching the club's youngsters before in the summer of 1973 he teamed up again with Harry Potts as Blackpool's youth coach before later returning to Turf Moor as youth team manager.

POINTS

Under the three points for a win system which was introduced in 1981682, Burnley's best points tally is the 83 points gained in 1991-92 when the club won the Fourth Division Championship. The club's best points haul under the old two points for a win system is 62 achieved in 1972-73 when the Clarets won the Second Division Championship. Under the present rule that would mean 86 points.

Burnley's lowest points record in the Football League occurred in 1889-90 when only 13 points were secured. That was from a 22-match programme and the club's lowest from a 42-match programme is 27 points in seasons 1970-71 and 1979-80 when the club were relegated on each occasion.

POTTS, HARRY

Burnley's most successful manager, Harry Potts was one of the first products of the club's youth policy. He joined the Turf Moor club in November 1937 but just as he looked likely to make a big impact in the game, war broke out. He spent a large part of the war with the RAF in the Far East and in 1945 was a member of Denis Compton's star-studded team which toured India. He also 'guested' for Sunderland and Fulham in the Second World War, netting 10 goals in 11 games for the Craven Cottage club.

He made his Football League debut in the opening game of the 1946-47 season, a 1-1 draw against Coventry City. That campaign saw Potts top score with 15 goals in 40 games as the Clarets won promotion to the First Division. The club also reached the FA Cup Final only to lose 1-0 to Charlton Athletic. Potts top scored again in 1947-48 and again in 1949-50 when he netted his only hat-trick for the club in a 5-1 defeat of Everton. After scoring 50 goals in 181 games, Potts left Turf Moor in October 1950 to join Everton before being appointed chief coach at Wolverhampton Wanderers in July 1956. A year later he took over as manager of Shrewsbury Town before taking charge of Burnley in January 1958.

After inheriting the nucleus of a fine side, he led the Clarets to the League Championship in 1959-60 with 56 points, two ahead of Wolves. Burnley also reached the FA Cup Final in 1962 only to lose 3-1 to Spurs. The previous season they had lost to Spurs in the semi-final. They entered European football for the first time and gave a good account of themselves in the European Cup. Burnley also reached the semi-final of the League Cup but lost to Aston Villa in the third game.

When Potts sold Jimmy McIlroy to Stoke City for £25,000, many fans were so angry that they refused to attend Turf Moor for the club's home games. With attendances dwindling, Potts was forced to sell Burnley's star players and over the years the heart was ripped out of the club by the sale of John Connelly, Alex Elder, Willie Irvine, Andy Lochhead and Willie Morgan.

In February 1970 Potts became the club's general manager, ending 12 years of the most successful period in Burnley's history. He left Turf Moor in July 1972 but the following year took over the reins at

Blackpool. Though the Seasiders were always challenging for a place in the top flight they never made it and in May 1976 he lost his job.

Two months later he returned to Turf Moor as chief scout before again being appointed Burnley manager in February 1977. In 1978-79 the club won the Anglo-Scottish Cup but after a poor start to the 1979-80 season, he was sacked. He later scouted for the new defunct Colne Dynamoes.

PROMOTION

Burnley have been promoted on seven occasions. The club were first promoted in 1897-98 when after winning the Second Division Championship, they participated in the Test Matches against Blackburn Rovers, Newcastle United and Stoke. After each team had played three games, Burnley met Stoke at the Victoria Ground. With both clubs on four points, the game ended as a goalless draw and both clubs played First Division football the following season.

Burnley's next experience of promotion was 1912-13 as they finished runners-up in the Second Division to Preston North End, three points behind the champions. It was an eventful season as the Clarets also reached the semi-final of the FA Cup where they lost to Sunderland in a replay.

It was 1946-47 before the club won promotion again, finishing four points behind champions Manchester City. The Clarets were unlucky to have missed out on a Cup and promotion double when they lost 1-0 after extra-time to Charlton Athletic in the FA Cup Final. The club were promoted for a fourth time in 1972-73. After winning seven and drawing nine of their opening 16 fixtures, the Clarets lost just four games in winning the Second Division Championship.

When Burnley won promotion for a fifth time in 1981-82 as they won the Third Division Championship, it was all the more remarkable as they had lost six of their opening eight fixtures!

The club's sixth experience of promotion was in 1991-92 when they won the Fourth Division Championship after spending seven seasons in the League's basement. Burnley last gained promotion in 1993-94 when after finishing sixth in the 'new' Division Two, they beat Plymouth Argyle and Stockport County in the play-offs to win a place in the First Division for the following season.

Q

QUICKEST GOALS

The club's early records do not include precise goal times and so it is impossible to state accurately the Clarets' quickest goalscorer. However, there is no doubt which match had the greatest number of early goals. When Burnley met Manchester United on 9 January 1954 in a third round FA Cup tie, Les Shannon shot the Clarets ahead in the opening seconds. The home side went 2-0 up within the first minute through Bill Holden before United pulled a goal back when Dennis Viollet converted Ernie Taylor's cross. Barely five minutes had been played when the Clarets' full-back Jock Aird turned the ball past his own 'keeper to level the scores! Burnley regained the lead just before half time and went on to win the tie 5-3.

R

RAPID SCORING

When Burnley won the Second Division Championship in 1897-98 they beat Loughborough Town 9-3 – still the highest number of goals ever scored in a Football League match involving the Clarets. Jimmy Ross netted a hat-trick inside the first 14 minutes and after quarter-of-an-hour Tom Morrison made it 4-0. After the visitors had pulled a goal back, Ross got his fourth and Burnley's fifth goal. Just before half-time, further strikes from Toman and Taylor gave Burnley a 7-1 lead at the interval. Ferguson and Ross again scored within minutes of the restart before Loughborough managed a little respectability with two late goals.

RECEIPTS

The club's record receipts are £150,000 for the FA Cup fourth round tie against Liverpool at Turf Moor on 28 January 1995.

RELEGATION

Burnley have suffered relegation on nine occasions. Their first experience was in 1896-97 when after finishing bottom of the First Division, the club were involved in the Test Matches, the results of which saw them lose their top flight status. In 1899-1900 the Turf moor club needed to win their last game at Nottingham Forest but went down 4-0. The Nottingham officials later claimed that Burnley 'keeper Jack Hillman had offered a bribe to the Forest players if they would let Burnley win. Though he claimed he was joking, the Football League suspended him for the whole of the following season. The club were relegated for a third time in 1929-30 when despite winning their last game of the season 6-2 against Derby County, the club went down on goal average.

It was 1970-71 before the Clarets were relegated again after 24 years in the First Division. Goals were hard to come by and they failed to score in half of their 42 matches and Eric Probert was top scorer with five goals! The Clarets were relegated for a fifth time in 1975-76 after winning promotion three seasons earlier. Again goals were in short supply and the club lost their top flight status after losing 1-0 at home to Manchester United in the penultimate game of the season.

In 1979-80 the Clarets were relegated to the Third Division after they failed to win any of their last 16 games. Promotion was achieved two seasons later but sadly in 1982-83 after just one season in Division Two, Burnley were relegated for a seventh time. In 1984-85, the Clarets were relegated to the League's basement for the first time in their history. Two seasons later they almost lost their League status but beat Orient 2-1 on the final day of the season. The club's last experience of relegation came in 1994-95 when they finished 22nd in the 'new8 First Division.

ROBSON, JIMMY

After a number of impressive performances in the club's Central League side, inside-forward Jimmy Robson was given his league debut in October 1956 when he scored in a 2-2 home draw against Blackpool. Over the next two seasons, Robson appeared in just four league games before establishing himself in the Clarets' first team in 1958-59. That season he scored 10 goals in 33 games including a hat-trick in a 3-1 win at Chelsea. At the end of the campaign, Robson was selected for the England Under-23 side and scored in a 2-2 draw against West Germany. When Burnley won the League Champion-

Jimmy Robson, scorer of five goals against Nottingham Forest during Burnley's League Championship winning season of 1959-60.

ship in 1959-60, Robson scored 18 goals in 38 games including five in the 8-0 demolition of Nottingham Forest.

In 1960-61, Robson topped the club's scoring charts with 25 goals including hat-tricks against Preston North End (Home 5-0) Fulham (Home 5-0) and Chelsea (Away 6-2) in the space of 46 days. At the end of that season he played for the FA XI against Spurs in the FA Charity Shield. When Burnley lost 3-1 to the White Hart Lane club in the FA Cup Final of 1962, Robson scored the Clarets' goal. He took his tally of goals for the Turf Moor club to exactly 100 in 242 League and Cup gamers before being transferred to Blackpool for £10,000.

He spent three years at Bloomfield Road, scoring 14 goals in 64 games but following the Seasiders relegation, he joined Barnsley, helping the Oakwell club win promotion. Robson later ended his league career with Bury before returning to Turf Moor as the youth team coach. He later managed Bacup Borough before being appointed to the Rochdale coaching staff.

RODAWAY, BILLY

A former England Schoolboy international, Billy Rodaway made his Burnley debut as a replacement for Colin Waldron in a 1-0 home win over Preston North End on 25 April 1972. He kept his place for the final game of the campaign as the Clarets beat Portsmouth 2-1. Despite two outstanding performances he didn't appear at all during the 1972-73 season and in fact, it was 1974-75 before he won a regular place. Forming a good understanding with Jim Thomson, he was ever-present in 1976-77 as Burnley finished 16th in Division Two.

He left Turf Moor in July 1981 to join Peterborough United, making 81 league appearances for 'The Posh' before spells at Blackpool and Tranmere Rovers.

He returned to play for Burnley just before the start of the infamous 1986-87 season, taking his tally of appearances to 305, the last of which was the 'Orient' game. On leaving the club a second time, he played non-League football for Runcorn and Altrincham before joining Colne Dynamoes and appearing in the FA Vase Final victory over Emley in 1988

S

SCOTT, DEREK

Derek Scott was born in Gateshead and won England Schoolboy hon-

Derek Scott, son-in-law of Burnley stalwart Brian Miller.

ours before joining Burnley as an apprentice, becoming a full-timer in February 1975. He made his debut in a 2-0 defeat at Manchester City in the penultimate game of the 1974-75 season though it was towards the end of the following campaign before he established himself as the club's first-choice right-back. After the emergence of Brian Laws, Scott was switched to midfield and in 1980-81, netted 11 goals in 38 games. The following season he helped the Clarets win the Third Division Championship and though they were relegated in 1982-83, they reached the semi-finals of the League

Cup. In the semi-final second-leg against Liverpool, Scott scored the game's only goal but the Clarets had lost the first leg at Anfield 3-0.

Scott had scored 31 goals in 364 games for Burnley when he joined Bolton for £20,000 prior to the start of the 1985-86 season. In his first season at Burnden Park, he made a Wembley appearance in the Freight Rover Trophy Final and was the club's regular right-back. Relegation to the Fourth Division in 1987 meant that he had appeared in all four divisions of the League. He helped the Wanderers win promotion in 1987-88 but at the end of the season was given a free transfer and joined Northern Premier League First Division side, Colne Dynamoes.

SECOND DIVISION

Burnley have had eight spells in the Second Division. Their first lasted just one season, for in 1897-98 after winning the Second Division Championship, the club won promotion to the top flight via the Test Matches. The club's second and longest spell in the Second Division began in 1900-01 and lasted for 13 seasons. In that first season, Burnley were unbeaten at home, winning 15 and drawing two of their fixtures but could only finish third. They finished third again in 1911-12 before winning promotion the following season. Burnley's third spell in Division Two lasted for ten seasons either side of the Second World War before the Clarets won promotion to the First Division in 1946-47. After 24 seasons of top flight football, Burnley lost their First Division status in 1970-71 and spent two seasons in Division Two before winning the Championship. After three seasons in Division One, the Clarets found themselves back in the Second Division but after three seasons of mid-table placings, they were relegated to the Third Division. Burnley's sixth spell in the Second Division lasted just one season after which they returned to Division Three.

Following reorganisation in 1992-93, the club found themselves in the 'new' Division Two but after two seasons won promotion to the First Division. Sadly after just one season, the Clarets were back in the Second Division and at the time of writing have spent their last four seasons in that section.

SEITH, BOBBY

The son of a former Scottish League player, Bobby Seith made his Burnley debut in a 2-1 win at Manchester United in October 1953, after having joined the club from Monifieth Tayside. After first displacing Jimmy Adamson in the Burnley side, Seith settled down to become a first team regular for the next seven seasons, scoring six goals in 238 games. Sadly he lost his place in the Clarets' side during the club's run-in to the League title in 1959-60 and, after a clash with Chairman Bob Lord, was transfer listed and refused a full-deserved Championship medal.

He then joined Dundee and in 1961-62 helped the Dens Park club win the Scottish League Championship. After hanging up his boots, he joined Dundee's coaching staff, later moving to Rangers in a similar capacity. Seith became manager of Preston North End in 1967 but in 1969-70 they finished bottom of Division Two and he gave way to Alan Ball senior. He later managed Hearts, taking them to a semi-final of the Scottish Cup in 1974. However, after a terrible start to the 1974-75 season, he resigned.

SEMI-FINALS

Up to the end of the 1998-99 season, Burnley have been involved in eight FA Cup semi-finals and three Football League Cup semi-finals.

SHANNON, LES

After an outstanding display for the Central League's representative side against Burnley in October 1949, Les Shannon, who scored his side's goal in a 2-1 defeat, left Liverpool after failing to make much headway. He joined Burnley for a fee of £4,000 and though he made his debut in a 2-0 defeat at Blackpool in December 1949, it was 1951-52 before he won a regular place in the Clarets' side.

The following season he was ever-present as Burnley finished the campaign in sixth place in the First Division. That season was his best in terms of goals scored, his total of 15 included two hat-tricks in victories over West Bromwich Albion (Home 5-0) and Tottenham Hotspur (Home 3-2). When Reg Attwell left the club, Shannon switched to wing-half and though he had played for England 'B' on three occasions, his performances in his new-found position led to him beings elected as a reserve for the Football League side.

Shannon went on to score 44 goals in 281 League and Cup games before following coaching spells at Everton and Arsenal, he became manager of Bury. He helped the Shakers win promotion in 1967-68 but after the club were relegated the following season, he left Gigg Lane. In May 1969 he took over the reins at Blackpool and steered the Seasiders to promotion to the First Division in his first season with the club. He parted company with the Bloomfield Road club early the following season and spent many years coaching in Greece.

SHERPA VAN TROPHY

The competition for Associate Members of the Football League was first sponsored for the 1987-88 season by Sherpa Van.

Burnley won both their group matches, beating Tranmere Rovers at Prenton Park 2-1 and Rochdale 3-2 with Neil Grewcock scoring in both matches. A George Oghani goal was enough to beat Chester City in the first round, whilst a Paul Comstive penalty accounted for Bury at Gigg Lane in round two. After a goalless draw against Halifax Town in the Northern Area semi-final, the Clarets won 5-3 in the resultant penalty shoot-out. In the Northern Area Final, Burnley met Preston North End. After a goalless draw in the first leg at Turf Moor, the Clarets won the return match at Deepdale 3-1 after the game had gone into extra-time. A crowd of 80,841 were present at Wembley Stadium for the final against Wolverhampton Wanderers. Andy Farrell almost put the Clarets ahead in the opening minute but his diving header went wide of the upright. Wolves took the lead in the 22nd minute through Andy Mutch and scored a second six minutes into the second-half through Robbie Dennison. Burnley threw caution to the wind and Paul Comstive twice came close to scoring. His header grazed the crossbar, whilst a shot from the left-footed midfielder beat the Wolves 'keeper only for Andy Thompson to clear off the line. But it wasn't to be and Wolves took the trophy after Burnley failed to get the goals they fully deserved.

In 1988-89, the Clarets again won both group games, defeating York City (Away 2-0) and Hartlepool United (Home 3-0) with Brendan O'Connell scoring in both matches. In the first round,

Burnley drew 1-1 at home to Crewe Alexandra but lost 4-2 on penalties.

SMALLEST PLAYER

Although such statistics are always unreliable for those playing around the turn of the century, it appears that the distinction of being the Clarets' smallest player goes to one of the following – Brian Flynn, Ashley Hoskin, Johnny Price – all of whom measured around the 5ft 3ins mark.

SMELT, LEN

Full-back Len Smelt began his Football League career with Gainsborough Trinity. During the First World War he 'guested' for his home-town team, Rotherham County, Leeds City and Burnley before joining the Clarets on professional forms in March 1919.

He made his debut in a 2-0 defeat at Notts County on the opening day of the 1919-20 season, a campaign in which he was ever-present as the club were runners-up in the First Division. The following season he helped Burnley win the League Championship. Over the next four seasons, Smelt missed very few matches and was ever-present in 1922-23. On 17 November 1923, he played in his 100th consecutive match for the club and was made captain for the day as Burnley beat West Ham United 5-1. He went on to appear in 248 games for the Clarets and after a season coaching the club's 'A' team, he joined Barrow where he ended his playing days.

In 1932 he returned to Turf Moor as a member of the club's coaching staff but within six months, the popular defender had died, aged 47.

SMITH, CECIL

Wrexham-born Cecil Smith played his early football with Oswestry and Welshpool before signing for his home-town club. After two seasons with the Robins in which he was leading scorer, he left the Racecourse Ground to join Wigan Borough. He spent three seasons with the then Third Division (North) club but after they lost their League status he joined Notts County for a brief spell.

Smith then decided to try his luck in non-league football, first with

Macclesfiled and then with Stalybridge Celtic, for whom he established a club goalscoring record in 1931-32 when he netted 77 goals!

Not surprisingly, this marksmanship led to a number of clubs showing an interest in him, but it was Burnley who signed him in the summer of 1932 as they sought a replacement for the prolific George Beel. He made his debut in a 1-1 draw against Chesterfield on the opening day of the 1932-33 season and ended the campaign as the club's joint-top scorer with Tommy Jones, both players netting 16 goals. His total included his first hat-trick for the club in a 4-0 home win over West Ham United. The following season he topped the club's scoring charts with 17 goals and though he missed much of 1934-35 through injury, he returned in 1935-36 to once again head the club's scoring list, netting another hat-trick in a 3-0 defeat of Barnsley.

Smith, who had scored 54 goals in 119 games lost his place to a young Tommy Lawton and left Turf Moor in 1936 to end his league career with Cardiff City.

SMITH, DICK

One of the club's most prolific goalscorers during their Second Division days in the early part of the century, Dick Smith scored on his debut in a 2-0 win at Doncaster Rovers following his arrival from Workington. Though he only netted eight goals in that campaign, they included the first of five hat-tricks for the club in a 5-0 home win over Burslem Port Vale. After a disappointing season in 1905-06 he formed a prolific partnership with Arthur Bell and in February 1908 he scored hat-tricks in successive matches as the Clarets beat Barnsley (Home 4-1) and Chesterfield (Away 4-2). That season, Smith topped the club's scoring charts with 24 goals in 36 games. Smith headed the scoring lists again in 1908-09, his total of 18 goals including four against Gainsborough Trinity (Home 5-2) and a hat-trick in the 9-0 demolition of Crystal Palace in an FA Cup second round replay.

Smith who had scored 76 goals in 185 League and Cup games lost his first team place midway through the 1909-10 season and at the end of that campaign returned to live in Workington.

SPONSORS

The club's present sponsors are Endsleigh Insurance. Burnley's previous sponsors have included Multipart, T.S.B and Polo.

STEVENSON, ALAN

Goalkeeper Alan Stevenson began his league career with his home-town club, Chesterfield, winning a Fourth Division Championship medal with them in 1969-70, his first season at the club. His performances for the Spireites earned him international recognition and he was capped at Under-23 level before joining Burnley for £50,000 in January 1972.

Alan Stevenson, holder of the club's record for clean sheets, keeping 18 in 1980-81.

He made his debut in a 1-0 defeat at Orient, going on to appear in 89 consecutive league games thereafter. During that period he helped Burnley win the Second Division Championship in 1972-73, keeping 18 clean sheets. Stevenson was the club's first-choice 'keeper for 11 seasons and was ever-present in 1972-73, 1977-78, 1978-79 and 1981-82. He helped the club win the Third Division Championship in 1982-82, again keeping 18 clean sheets. Stevenson appeared in 543 League and Cup games for the Clarets before leaving to join Rotherham United. After a season at Millmoor, he played for Hartlepool United later being appointed the club's commercial manager. He went on to hold a similar post with both Middlesborough and West Bromwich Albion before taking on the same role with Huddersfield Town.

STOCKPORT COUNTY

On 26 January 1991, Burnley and Stockport County met for the 11th time in League and Cup games in exactly 17 months. The breakdown of first-class matches was four Division Four, three Leyland DAF Cup, two FA Cup and two Rumbelows Cup games.

Between 8 and 26 January 1991, they met three times, the last two encounters within four days when Burnley won successive games 3-2 in the Leyland Daf Cup and Fourth Division. Burnley won four games, County three and there were four draws.

STRONG, JIMMY

Goalkeeper Jimmy Strong made his league debut for Hartlepool United before going on to play for both Chesterfield and Portsmouth prior to the Second World War. He had signed for Walsall in the summer of 1939 but the hostilities ended any hopes he had of playing for the Saddlers. During the war he 'guested' for Blackpool and Rochdale before playing for the Clarets in a similar capacity. He joined Burnley on a permanent basis in January 1946 and after making his debut in the 1-1 home draw against Coventry City on the opening day of the 1946-47 season, went on to appear in 203 consecutive league games.

During the course of that sequence, Strong helped the club win promotion to the top flight and appeared in the 1947 FA Cup Final whilst in 1947-48 he was in splendid form as the Clarets finished third in Division One. Strong went on to appear in 285 League and Cup games before losing his place to Des Thompson who had joined the club from York City.

On his retirement, Strong, one of the club's most consistent 'keepers, ran his own poultry farm on the outskirts of town.

SUBSTITUTES

The first-ever Burnley substitute was Ian Towers who came on for Willie Irvine in the 2-2 home draw against Arsenal on 28 August 1965. The club had to wait another two seasons for their first goalscoring substitute – Willie Irvine scored the Clarets' goal in a 1-1 draw at home to Nottingham Forest on 7 October 1967. The greatest number of substitutes used in a single season by Burnley under the single substitute rule was 30 in 1985-86. From 1986-87 two substitutes were allowed and in the 1994-95 season, the club used 67. For the last few seasons, three substitutes have been allowed and in 1997-98, 88 were used. The greatest number of substitute appearances for the Clarets has been made by John Francis who was brought on during 34 league games and 11 Cup ties. It was Francis who rewrote the Burnley records on the matter of substitutes with an extraordinary 18 appearances in the substitute's shirt in 1995-96.

SUSPENSIONS

When Burnley played their last league game of the 1899-1900 season, they needed to beat Nottingham Forest to save them from relegation to Division Two. Unfortunately they were beaten 4-0. Goalkeeper Jack Hillman was Burnley's captain and after the match, Forest alleged that he offered their captain £2 a man to take the match easy. The complaint was lodged by letter to the FA. At the interval, Burnley were two goals down and during the break, Hillman was alleged to have approached his opposite number and offered to increase the bribe to £5 a man. Hillman admitted that the text of the complaint was true but that he did not knowingly and with intent make an offer to the Forest team to take it easy. He maintained that this conversation was all chaff and arose out of an episode two weeks previously in which some suspicion had been thrown on the Forest club after losing 8-0 at West Bromwich Albion, a side they had earlier beaten 6-1.

Hillman was suspended for the whole of the 1900-01 season. It was not the first time he had been in trouble for in 1897-98 whilst playing for Dundee, who were almost bankrupt, he was suspended for allegedly not trying, but there was a suspicion that the club could not afford to pay his wages of £4 a week. Hillman lost his case and was transferred to Burnley for £130.

SUSTAINED SCORING

In 1927-28 George Beel, the club's leading scorer, netted 35 goals in 39 league games. He scored two hat-tricks in wins over Derby County (Home 4-2) and Sheffield United (Home 5-3) and hit seven 'doubles' yet despite his prolific marksmanship, the club were nearly relegated, finishing 19th in Division One.

SUTCLIFFE, ARTHUR

Arthur Sutcliffe was Burnley's secretary when in 1893 he was asked to combine his duties with that of becoming the club's first team manager. Previously the Burnley side had been selected by a committee.

The club's policy of bringing Scottish players to Turf Moor continued under Sutcliffe's leadership but after taking the club to fifth place in Division One in his first season in charge, the club slipped to ninth the following campaign. In 1895-96, Sutcliffe's last season as the club's team manager, Burnley finished tenth and at the end of the campaign he relinquished his position and left the club.

T

TALLEST PLAYERS

It is impossible to say for definite who has been the tallest player ever on Burnley's books as such records are notoriously unreliable. Players who can lay claim to the title are Ian Helliwell, Bob Johnson and David Jones who all stand around 6ft 3ins, whilst John Gayle is credited in the Rothman's Yearbook as 6ft 4ins.

TAYLOR, DAVID

Born in Bannockburn, left-back David Taylor played his early football for Motherwell and Glasgow Rangers before joining Bradford City in October 1910. At the end of his first season with the Yorkshire club he won an FA Cup winners' medal as they beat Newcastle United 1-0. Six months later he joined Burnley and made his debut in a 1-1 draw at Huddersfield Town. He was a virtual ever-present in the four seasons leading to the First World War and in 1914 won a second FA Cup winners' medal as the Clarets beat Liverpool 1-0.

One of the fastest full-backs in the Football League, he found the competition for first team places much stiffer after the hostilities and after playing in the opening nine games of the club's League Championship winning season of 1920-21, lost his place to Len Smelt.

He went on to appear in 250 League and Cup games before returning to Scotland to manage St Johnstone. He later had a spell coaching

Blackburn Rovers before returning to management with Carlisle United.

TAYLOR, JOE

During his early playing days, Burnley-born Joe Taylor was a prolific goalscorer but on joining Bacup Borough he switched from the forwards to play in the half-back line. He joined Burnley in November 1893 but had to wait until midway through the following season before making his league debut for the club in a 4-0 defeat at Preston North End. He appeared in just six games that campaign before becoming a virtual ever-present over the next 12 seasons. Having scored just two goals in his first three seasons with the club, he netted three in the opening four games of the 1897-98 season as the Clarets went on to win the Second Division Championship.

The first Burnley player to make 300 league appearances for the club, he had scored 14 goals in 352 League and Cup games when he hung up his boots at the end of the 1906-07 season.

TAYLOR, STEVE

Steve Taylor began his Football League career with Bolton Wanderers and made his debut as a substitute in a 2-1 defeat at Bristol City in September 1974. In 1976-77 he formed a prolific goalscoring partnership with Neil Whatmore, who also later played for the Clarets, scoring 16 goals in 31 games as the Wanderers finished fourth in Division Two and reached the League Cup semi-finals.

The much-travelled striker had spells with Port Vale, Oldham Athletic, Luton Town and Mansfield Town before joining Burnley for £35,000 in the summer of 1980. His first game for the club was in a 1-1 home draw against Newport County, Taylor going on to be the Clarets' top scorer with 16 goals including a hat-trick in a 5-0 home win over Millwall. He won a Third Division Championship medal in 1981682 following a good partnership with Billy Hamilton, especially in the first half of the season. He continued to find the net in 1982-83, scoring hat-tricks in a 4-1 win over Sheffield Wednesday and a 7-1 defeat of Charlton Athletic. That season also saw Burnley meet Sheffield Wednesday in the FA Cup sixth round but with the teams level at 1-1, Taylor missed a penalty and the Owls won the re-play 5-0!

Taylor left Turf Moor in August 1983 and joined Wigan Athletic, later playing for Stockport County, Rochdale, and Preston North End before rejoining Burnley in the summer of 1987. He played in the Sherpa Van Trophy Final and took his tally of goals to 52 in 181 games before rejoining Rochdale for a second spell. After hanging up his boots, he became manager of non-League Mossley.

TERNENT, STAN

Burnley manager Stan Ternent began his league career with the Clarets, making his debut in a 7-0 defeat at Sheffield Wednesday in May 1967. After making just five first team appearances, Ternent was transferred to Carlisle United for £4,000 and went on to make 188 league appearances for the Cumbrian side, helping them reach the First Division in 1973-74. At the end of that season he joined Sunderland but after failing to break into the Wearsiders' first team, he joined Blackpool as coach.

In August 1979 he replaced Bob Stokoe as the Seasiders' manager, though his time in charge was brief. With the club in the bottom half of the Third Division, he was relieved of his duties. After a spell coaching Bradford City, he became assistant-manager to Crystal Palace's Steve Coppell, later being appointed manager of Hull City. He was dismissed from Boothferry Park in early 1991 and after helping Mike Walsh at Bury, became the Shakers' manager on Walsh's departure. He led the Gigg Lane club to two consecutive promotions, culminating in a place in the First Division for the 1996-97 season. Surprisingly he was replaced by Neil Warnock in the 1998 close season, later being appointed manager of Burnley. In what was a difficult first season for the Burnley boss, he led the Clarets to 15th place in the Second Division.

TEST MATCHES

Burnley were twice involved in the Test Matches. In 1896-97 they finished bottom of the First Division and were involved in matches against the top two clubs from the Second Division, namely Newton Heath and Notts County. They beat Newton Heath 2-0 at home but lost by the same scoreline away before drawing 1-1 at Notts County and losing 1-0 at home to the Meadow Lane club. These results cost the Clarets their place in the top flight. The following season, Burnley won the Second Division Championship but were not promoted automatically and had to play

Test Matches against Stoke, Newcastle United and Blackburn Rovers. On Thursday 28 April 1898, Blackburn Rovers had beaten Newcastle 4-3, leaving both Stoke and Burnley on four points and Newcastle on two points. Stoke and Burnley players knew therefore that a draw in their match at the Victoria Ground on the following Saturday would be sufficient to keep Stoke in the First Division and lift Burnley out of the Second.

Despite the fact that everyone knew an 'arrangement' was in the offing, Stoke and Burnley made their intentions so patently obvious that they gave the League no choice but to revamp the 'Test Match' or drop it completely. The game proved a complete fiasco reported 'The Staffordshire Advertiser'. 'Athletic News' called it a fraud. "The teams could have done without a goalkeeper, so anxious were the forwards not to score." Played in wet and windy conditions on a shocking pitch, the players kicked the ball into the crowd so often that the disgruntled fans 'gave themselves up to unlimited fun with the ball on their own account'. To stop this happening for the umpteenth time, one of the linesmen tried so hard to stop the ball reaching the crowd that he ran headlong into a policeman who went head over heels!

The final table read:

	P.	W.	D.	L.	F.	A.	Pts
Burnley	4	2	1	1	5	3	5
Stoke	4	2	1	1	4	2	5
Newcastle United	4	2	0	2	9	6	4
Blackburn Rovers	4	1	0	3	5	12	2

TEXACO CUP

The predecessor of the Anglo-Scottish Cup, it was launched in 1970-71 and was for English, Irish and Scottish club sides not involved in European competition.

The club's first opponents in the competition were Heart of

Midlothian who the Clarets beat 3-1 in the first leg at Turf Moor. However, in a disastrous return match at Tynecastle, Burnley lost 4-1 to crash out of the competition at the first hurdle 5-4. When the club entered the competition for a second time in 1973-74, they went all the way to the final. In the first round, Burnley beat East Fife 7-0 at home with Paul Fletcher netting a hat-trick and 3-2 at Bayview Park to complete a 10-2 aggregate win over the hapless Scots. In round two, the Clarets gained revenge for their defeat at the hands of Hearts in 1970-71 with a comprehensive 8-0 aggregate win. In the third round, Burnley met Norwich City and after winning the first leg at Turf Moor 2-0, went on to reach the final with a 5-2 aggregate win. In the final, Burnley faced Newcastle United at St James Park. After 90 minutes the teams were level at 1-1 with Paul Fletcher having scored for the Clarets but a goal late into extra-time gave the Magpies the cup.

THIRD DIVISION

Burnley have had two spells in the Third Division. Following relegation in 1979-80, Burnley began their first-ever season in the Third Division with a 1-1 home draw against Newport County and ended the campaign in eighth place. In 1981-82, the Clarets won the Third Division Championship, despite losing six of their first eight matches. However, during the course of the season, they strung together a 20-match unbeaten run and took the title on goal difference from Carlisle United.

The club's second spell in the Third Division, which began in 1983-84 after just one campaign in Division Two, also lasted two seasons. After finishing 12th in 1983-84, the Clarets were relegated to the Fourth Division the following season after finishing 21st, their lowest-ever league placing at that time.

THOMAS, DAVE

Burnley's youngest-ever top flight player, Dave Thomas played his first game for the club in a 1-1 draw at home to Everton on the final day of the 1966-67 season at the age of 16 years 220 days. The following season he helped the Clarets win the FA Youth Cup before winning a regular first team place in 1968-69. His performances led to him winning international recognition at England Under-23 level despite still being well short of his 20th birthday. For Burnley, Thomas scored 23 goals in 179 games before being sold to the club's Second Division promotion rivals, Queen's Park Rangers for £165,000. Able to play on either flank, Thomas was part of the Rangers' team who were promoted to Division One and was a regular choice in the side that finished runners-up in the First Division in 1976. Very fast and an excellent crosser of the ball, he earned eight caps for England whilst playing for Rangers.

Everton were one of a number of clubs interested in signing Thomas and in August 1977 they completed the transfer for a fee of £200,000. In his first season at Goodison Park, Thomas provided the crosses from which Bob Latchford scored the majority of his 30 goals. Thomas only stayed for two seasons before leaving to join Wolverhampton Wanderers. Never really settling at Molineux, he had a spell with Vancouver Whitecaps before returning to play for Middlesbrough. Thomas ended his league career with Portsmouth where he became youth team coach.

THOMSON, HARRY

Goalkeeper Harry Thomson joined the Clarets from Edinburgh and District League side Bo'ness United in August 1959. Because of the consistency of Scottish international 'keeper Adam Blacklaw, Thomson had to wait six seasons before making his first team debut. That came in March 1965 as the Clarets won 2-0 at Leicester City, with Thomson making a penalty save during the course of the game. He began the 1965-66 season as the club's first-choice 'keeper but a broken hand let Blacklaw back into the side. He regained his place midway through the following season and in February 1967 played what was without doubt his greatest game for the club.

Burnley had beaten Napoli 3-0 at Turf Moor in the first leg of the Fairs Cup third round match and so knew they would have to defend in depth at the San Paulo Stadium. Harry Thomson saved a penalty and made a series of outstanding saves as the game finished 0-0. His performance led to one Italian newspaper likening him to "A God in a green jersey". At the end of that season he was invited to tour with the Scottish FA and represented his country for the first time against Israel in Tel Aviv in May 1967.

Thomson made 141 appearances for Burnley before being transferred to Blackpool following the arrival of Peter Mellor. He loved to play to the crowd and with both Burnley and Blackpool he was censured for his on-field antics! He appeared in 68 games for the Seasiders before ending his league career with Barrow in the Fourth Division.

THOMSON, JIM

Glasgow-born Jim Thomson played his early football for local club Provenside Hibernian before signing for Chelsea in January 1965. He appeared in 39 games for the Stamford Bridge club before leaving to join Burnley for a fee of £40,000 in September 1968.

Playing his first game for the Clarets at right-back, he was given the run around by Liverpool's Peter Thompson as the Reds won 4-0 at Turf Moor. In his first four seasons with the club, Jim Thomson found it difficult to hold down a first team place but in 1972-73 after being moved to the heart of the defence, he was one of six ever-presents. That season the Clarets won the Second Division Championship and

with Colin Waldron partnering Thomson in the centre of defence, the club only conceded 35 goals.

Jim Thomson captained Burnley to success in the Anglo-Scottish Cup in 1978 but then the following season lost his place to Vince Overson. Thomson, whose Turf Moor career spanned three decades, appeared in 363 games before leaving to become player-coach at non-League Morecambe. After working in the brewery trade, he returned to Turf moor in the summer of 1986 as the club's Commercial Manager but left

Jim Thomson, Clarets' skipper when they won the Anglo-Scottish Cup in 1978.

in September 1987.

TRANSFERS

The club's record transfer fee received is the £750,000 that Luton Town paid for Steve Davis in August 1995. Burnley's record transfer fee paid is £350,000 to Birmingham City for the services of Paul Barnes in September 1996.

TURF MOOR

Formed in 1881 as Burnley Rovers rugby club, they took up football in May of the following year when they dropped the name Rovers. In February 1883 the club played its first game at Turf Moor when they entertained Rawtenstall, a match they lost 6-3. By 1885 the club had built a stand to seat 800 spectators, adapted 'a natural earthwork' to hold over 2,000 spectators and built two uncovered stands on wooden bleachers that could seat another 5,000 fans.

In October 1886, Turf Moor became the first football ground to be visited by royalty when Prince Albert who was in the town to open a hospital, went to see the Clarets' game against Bolton Wanderers, a match the visitors won 4-3.

In 1908 the club covered both the Main Stand and the Star Stand whilst a year later, the Cricket Field End terrace was covered.

Between the wars, the lower reaches of the Long Side, which had replaced the Star Stand, were terraced in concrete, though it was 1954 before the whole bank was covered. Three years later the club installed floodlights which were first switched on for a friendly against Blackburn Rovers on 16 December 1957.

In 1967/68, work began at the Cricket Ground End on an £180,000 stand, seating 4,500 spectators and housing all the players' facilities. The Stand which incorporated oil-fired heating for the fans was eventually opened in 1959, but within two years had to be shut down as it proved too costly. It was November 1975 before the Stand was belatedly opened by the Prime Minister Edward Heath. Shortly afterwards a new single-tier stand named the Bob Lord Stand was built, also opened by Edward Heath in September 1974. At this time, the only uncovered section of the ground was the Bee Hole End, named after a colliery which used to stand behind it.

The Long Side, the Football League's last great bank of side terracing was cleared in 1995 and replaced by the North Stand which can hold 8,000 spectators on two tiers. The Bee Hole too has been replaced by a two tier stand, leaving Turf Moor's capacity at 22,546.

UNDEFEATED

The Clarets have gone through a league season without losing a home match on three occasions – 1897-98, 1990-01, and 1911-12.

The club's longest undefeated sequence in the Football League is 30 matches between 6 September 1920 and 25 March 1921.

Burnley's longest run of undefeated home matches is 34 between 1 April 1911 and 4 January 1913.

UTILITY PLAYERS

A utility player is one of those particularly gifted footballers who can play in a number of different positions. Two of Burnley's earliest utility players were Bill McFettridge and Walter Place senior who always gave good accounts of themsleves in almost any position. Both were inspirational footballers who could coax the very best out of those around them.

Towards the end of the 1960s, players were encouraged to become more adaptable and to see their roles as less stereotyped. However, at the same time, much less attention came to be paid to the implication of wearing a certain numbered shirt and so some of the more versatile players came to wear almost all the different numbered shirts at some stage or another, although this did not necessarily indicate a vast variety of positions. Martin Dobson wore all the different numbered outfield shirts, whilst players such as Geoff Nulty, Mike Phelan and Andy Farrell also appeared in most outfield numbered shirts.

VICTORIES IN A SEASON – HIGHEST

In the 1991-92 season, Burnley won 25 of their 42 league fixtures, the highest number of wins in the club's history and won the Fourth Division Championship.

VICTORIES IN A SEASON – LOWEST

Burnley's poorest performances came in seasons 1896-97, 1902-03 and 1979-80 when they won only six matches. However, in 1896-97, the Clarets only played 30 matches and 34 in 1902-03 whilst in 1979-80, Burnley had a 42-match programme.

WADDLE, CHRIS

One of the game's most exciting players, Chris Waddle began his league career with New-castle United, who signed him from Tow Law Town. He made his debut for the Magpies in October 1980 and the following season was ever-present. In 1983-84 he was part of the New-castle side that won pro-motion to the First Division and remained a regular member of the squad for the next six seasons. But in the sum-mer of 1985, after scor-ing 52 goals in 190 first team appearances, he was sold to Tottenham Hotspur for £590,000 following a well-publicised dispute with Magpies' manager Jack Charlton. He had an

Chris Waddle, pictured in his Tottenham Hotspur days.

excellent second season at White Hart Lane as Spurs finished third in Division One and reached the FA Cup Final. Plagued by injury and a loss of form he had a disastrous 1987-88 but came back strongly to top the club's scoring lists. With Spurs facing financial problems, he was sold to French champions Marseilles for £4.25 million, a new record for an English player. With the French club he won three League Championship medals and reached the 1991 European Cup Final.

He joined Sheffield Wednesday in the summer of 1992 for £1 million and despite having played the last of his 62 internationals against Turkey in October 1991, he was voted the Football Writers' Association Player of the Year. Waddle later played for Bradford City and Sunderland before joining Burnley as player-manager in July 1997.

He made his debut for the Clarets in a 1-0 defeat at Watford on the opening day of the 1997-98 season and, though he was a virtual ever-present in the first half of the season, an injury reduced his appearances thereafter. His only goal for the club came in a 2-2 home draw against Bournemouth but sadly his performances on the field were affected by his managerial duties and in May 1998 he parted company with the club.

Colin Waldron, Burnley's youngest captain in the top flight.

WALDRON, COLIN

Tall, strong blond defender Colin Waldron began his career as an apprentice with Bury, turning professional in May 1966. After only 20 league games for the Shakers, he left Gigg Lane to join Chelsea but couldn't settle in London and returned to the north-west to play for Burnley who paid £30,000 for his services in October 1967.

He made his debut for the Clarets in a 2-2 draw at Southampton and over the next eight seasons, developed into one of the game's most forceful players. In 1968-69, his second season at Turf Moor, he was appointed club captain, the youngest in the top flight. When Burnley won the Second Division Championship in 1972-73, Waldron was one of six ever-presents, his strike at Preston North End on the final day of the season giving the Clarets the title. Though he lost the captaincy for a short period, he regained it when Martin Dobson left to play for Everton. Waldron went on to score 18 goals in 356 games for the Turf Moor club before leaving on a free transfer to join Manchester United in May 1976.

He had a very short stay at Old Trafford, moving north to Sunderland after only three outings in United's colours. Waldron tried his luck in the United States, playing for both Atlanta Chiefs and Tulsa Roughnecks. In October 1979 he joined Rochdale, ending his league career with the Spotland club before having another spell in America with Philadelphia Fury.

WARTIME FOOTBALL

In spite of the outbreak of the First World War in 1914, the major football leagues embarked upon their planned programme of matches for the ensuing season and these were completed on schedule at the end of April the following year when the Clarets finished fourth in Division One. With the season barely over, the Football League announced what had long been expected – that there would be no more league football until hostilities ceased. In place of the league system, an ad hoc Lancashire Section was established but many of the regular players were absent, either serving abroad or finding alternative employment to aid the war effort. The club's best season was 1915-16 when they won the Subsidiary Tournament and were runners-up in the Principal Tournament.

In complete contrast to the events of 1914, once war was declared on 3 September 1939, the Football League programme of 1929-40 was suspended and for a while there was no football of any description. In October 1939 the game continued on a regional basis and with many of the younger players already enlisting in the services, it was agreed that a 'guest' system would be allowed. Even so, some of the opposition was ridiculously weak, Burnley beating Carlisle United 8-0, Accrington Stanley 7-0 and Southport 7-3. The league was extended for the 1940-41 season but not all teams played an equal number of fixtures and positions were determined on goal average. The next season became even more complicated, being split into two parts. The Clarets were heavily beaten 9-0 by Blackpool but fared even worse in the second part of the season, losing 13-0 at Bloomfield Road! The next three seasons were similar with none of the matches being taken too seriously.

WATERFIELD, GEORGE

When the Clarets signed George Waterfield from non-League Mexborough Town in October 1923, he was a winger and he made his debut at outside-left in a 2-0 home win over Sheffield United. Midway through the following season he switched to left-back, a position that the club had failed to fill since David Taylor left to manage St Johnstone.

Waterfield was the club's first-choice left-back for the next 11 seasons, being ever-present in 1927-28. His consistency led to him winning full international honours when he played for England in a 3-3 draw against Wales at the Racecourse Ground.

He went on to appear in 394 League and Cup games for the Clarets and though he only scored five goals, the side never lost when he found the back of the net. He left Turf Moor in the summer of 1935 and spent a season with Crystal Palace before hanging up his boots.

WATNEY CUP

This was Britain's first commercially sponsored tournament and was a pre-season competition for the top two highest scoring teams in each division of the Football League the previous season. They could only compete if they had no other European involvement.

After beating Lincoln City 1-0, courtesy of a Leighton James goal, the Clarets went out of the competition, beaten 2-0 at Turf Moor by Bristol Rovers.

WATSON, BILLY

Wing-half Billy Watson joined Burnley from his home-town club Southport Central in March 1909 and went straight into the side for the home match against Leeds City which was goalless. It was his only appearance that season and it took him until the 1910-11 campaign before winning a regular place in the side.

He helped the club win promotion to the First Division in 1912-13 and the following season wore the Number 6 shirt as Burnley beat Liverpool 1-0 to lift the FA Cup. His consistency was rewarded with the first of three full international caps for England when he played in a 1-0 win over Scotland at Stamford Bridge in April 1913.

He was still the club's first choice left-half when League football resumed in 1919-20 and when the Clarets won the League Championship the following season, he was the only ever-present. Watson went on to score 20 goals in 380 games, making his last appearance in a goalless home draw against Everton in September 1924. At the end of that season he left Turf Moor and joined Accrington as first team coach. He later moved to Blackburn Rovers where he combined his duties of coaching with the captaincy of the club's 'A' team.

WEATHER CONDITIONS

Prior to the kick-off of the match against Blackburn Rovers on 12 December 1891, snow had fallen for more than two hours, making playing conditions difficult. Burnley had the wind at their backs and by half-time had raced into a 3-0 lead with goals from Nicol, Galbraith and Bowes. It appeared that Rovers were not going to come out for the second-half but eventually they did. During a memorable blizzard, the two captains were sent-off following a brief fight, to be followed by the rest of the Rovers' side except goalkeeper Herbie Arthur, half-frozen and blinded by the sleet. The Rovers' 'keeper stayed on to hold the fort against the whole Burnley team. The referee ordered the game to proceed and as Burnley kicked-off, Arthur at once claimed off-side. The referee allowed the appeal but Arthur hesitated so long in taking the free-kick that the official wisely declared the game at an end!

WEB SITE

Two internet World Wide Web sites of interest are:
   www.clarets.co.uk (the official club site)
And, for the Clarets Independent Supporters Association:
   www.users.globalnet.co.uk/~davewynne/

WHITTAKER, SPEN

Spence Whittaker known as 'Spen' was the club's first full-time team manager with director WR Thornton carrying out secretarial duties.

He introduced a number of new players to the team including Hugh Moffat, goalkeeper Jerry Dawson and Alex Leake from Aston Villa. The club's fortunes improved but in April 1910 tragedy struck. Whilst on his way to London to register a player, he fell from the carriage near Crewe and died instantly. A benefit match was arranged at Turf Moor with the proceeds of the match against Manchester United going to his family.

WOODRUFF, ARTHUR

The oldest player to appear in League football for Burnley since the Second World War, Arthur Woodruff joined the Clarets from Bradford City in the summer of 1936. He played his first game for the club in a 2-0 home win over Plymouth Argyle in the fifth game of the 1936-37 season. He was a virtual ever-present in the side in the three seasons leading up to the Second World War and when League football resumed after the hostilities, he was still a member of the Burnley side, although by now he had been moved to right-back.

In 1946-47 he helped the club win promotion to the First Division, missing just two games and played for the Clarets in the FA Cup Final defeat by Charlton Athletic. His performances in the Burnley defence led to him making two appearances for the Football League against the League of Ireland and the Irish League. He had played in 292 League and Cup games for Burnley when after losing his place to Jock Aird, he joined Workington as the club's player/assistant-manager. He later held a similar position at Northwich Victoria before coaching Tranmere Rovers.

WORST START

The club's worst-ever start to a season was in 1889-90. It took 18 matches to record the first victory of the season, drawing four and losing 13 of the opening fixtures. The run ended with a 7-0 win over Bolton Wanderers at Turf Moor on 1 March 1890. The Clarets then won four and drew one of their remaining matches to finish 11th in the Football League and had to apply for re-election.

'X'

In football 'x' traditionally stands for a draw. The club record for the number of draws in a season was in 1981/82 when they drew 17 of their matches.

XMAS DAY

There was a time when football matches were regularly played on Christmas Day but, in recent years, the game's authorities have dropped the fixture from their calendar. The Clarets first played a league game on Christmas Day in 1893 when goals from Buchanan (2) Bowes and Espie helped them beat Sheffield United 4-1. Burnley then went on to win eight and draw two of their next 10 league matches played on Christmas Day before losing for the first time in 1913 when Sunderland won 1-0 at Turf Moor. During that spell, Burnley played seven matches against Blackpool, winning five and drawing two. Their best result was a 5-1 win in 1909 when Ben Green scored a hat-trick.

On Christmas Day 1920, Joe Anderson scored four goals in a 6-0 defeat of Sheffield United, whilst four years later, the Clarets suffered their heaviest defeat in 38 league games played on this date when they lost 5-1 at home to Huddersfield Town. Liverpool provided the opposition in games at Turf Moor in 1926 and 1928. Burnley won both games 4-0 and 3-2 respectively with the club's top marksman George Beel scoring twice in each game.

Burnley played their last Christmas Day fixture in 1957 when goals from Cheesebrough and Pilkington helped defeat Manchester City 2-1.

YOUNGEST PLAYER

The youngest player to appear in a first-class fixture for Burnley is Tommy Lawton who played in the Second Division match against

Doncaster Rovers (Home 1-1) on 28 March 1936 when he was 16 years 174 days old.

YOUTH CUP

Burnley have reached the final of the FA Youth Cup on just one occasion. In 1967-68, the young Clarets beat Manchester United, Manchester City, Sheffield United and Everton to reach the two-legged final against Coventry City. The first leg at Highfield Road, watched by a crowd of 14,836 saw the Sky Blues win 2-1 but in the return at Turf Moor, the Clarets led by Mick Docherty won 2-0 to take the trophy 3-2 on aggregate.

Z

ZENITH

Few fans will argue over which moments have been the finest in the Burnley's history. After winning the FA Cup for the only time in the club's history in 1914, when a Bert Freeman goal was enough to beat Liverpool 1-0, the Clarets progress was halted by the First World War. In the first full season after the hostilities, the club finished runners-up in the First Division but in 1920-21 won the League Championship for the first time in their history, embarking on a 30-match unbeaten run which remains a top flight record today.

Also of interest:

FOOTBALL & WAR

Gerard Reid

When at war, supporters identify with their 'side' for reasons as diverse as class, religion, and patriotism. Sound familiar? In football, supporters' beliefs can result in conflicts that go far deeper than the actual 'game'. These are the games that this book is about. Chapters include: games where nations were in actual conflict (Argentina v England, and England v Ireland), and even games which were the direct cause of war (Honduras v El Salvador). This is the first book to explore this subject. £6.95

BLEAK AND BLUE:
22 years at the Manchester Academy of Football Farce

Craig Winstanley

An essential read for all Blues fans and for football fans everywhere, Bleak and Blue is a hugely entertaining record of the joys and misery of two decades of the history of Manchester City Football Club. A big book in every way, the author's fanzine-style writing covers all major games in minute detail, relentlessly pursuing a club which could again be a great football club.

"An essential book for all Blues fans; and for all football fans....It's a brilliant read, even if you know nothing - and don't care - about football SOUTH MANCHESTER REPORTER £8.95

COME ON CYMRU 2000!

Keith Haynes

The original COME ON CYMRU was the first book to give the complete picture of the rivalries between teams and the fervent Welsh pride in their football. This new edition takes Welsh football into the new millennium with the same blend of fanzine-style writing by fans of Welsh football for supporters of football (and Wales!) everywhere. This is how the critics greeted the first edition:

"A cracking read, something that Wales has been crying out for, and it's from the fans as well - great stuff!" GERT THOMAS – BBC RADIO WALES

"... Keith Haynes is the Welsh Nick Hornby, you won't put this book down until you've read it from cover to cover." FUTURE MAGAZINE

£6.95

All of our books are available through your local bookseller. In case of difficulty, or for a free catalogue, please contact:

SIGMA LEISURE, 1 SOUTH OAK LANE, WILMSLOW, CHESHIRE SK9 6AR.

Phone: 01625-531035;
Fax: 01625-536800.
E-mail: info@sigmapress.co.uk   Web site: http//www.sigmapress.co.uk
VISA and MASTERCARD welcome.